NEBRASKA TRIVIA

NEBRASKA TRIVIA

COMPILED BY GABE PARKS

Rutledge Hill Press®
Nashville, Tennessee

Published in Nashville, Tennessee, by Rutledge Hill Press®,
211 Seventh Avenue North, Nashville, Tennessee 37219.
Distributed in Canada by H. B. Fenn & Company, Ltd.,
34 Nixon Road, Bolton, Ontario L7E 1W2.

Typography by Compass Communications, Inc., Nashville, Tennessee.

Library of Congress Cataloging-in-Publication Data available

Parks, Gabe, 1921–
    Nebraska trivia / compiled by Gabe Parks.
        p.   cm.
    ISBN 1-55853-605-1 (pbk.)
    1. Nebraska—Miscellanea.   2. Questions and answers.
I. Title.
F666.5.P37   1998
978.2'0076—dc21   98-17242
                                                          CIP

Printed in the United States of America.
3 4 5 6 7 8 9 — 01 00 99

PREFACE

Non-Nebraskans who read this book may be surprised to learn that there is more to the state than the college football team. We do burst with pride about our five-time national championship team, but Nebraskans also take pride in many other aspects of their state. The list of the state's leaders who have made their mark on the national scene is formidable and includes such names as Warren Buffett, Henry Fonda, Willa Cather, Buffalo Bill, William Jennings Bryan, John J. Pershing, and Father Flanagan to name a few. There are many facts, some of them little-known, about these and many other important figures that appear in this book.

For readers who wish to have a little fun with some facts about Nebraska, this is the book for you. You can use it to impress your friends with your store of basic, sometimes mundane, often obscure, but always interesting information about this state. For those who have recently arrived in Nebraska, this book can provide a modest crash course on what the state is all about. For those who have left the state, it may help maintain a link to the place you once called home. And for those who have been Cornhuskers most of your lives, you may find questions that evoke memories. There may also be some paragraphs which will cause you to exclaim: "I didn't know that."

I've lived in this prairie state for more than fifty years, most of it spent in the news business. However, during my research for this book, my eyes were opened to a sheaf of Nebraska facts that were new to me. Perhaps the same thing will happen to you.

ACKNOWLEDGMENTS

I wish to thank these former colleagues at the *Omaha World-Herald* for their invaluable suggestions of topics and for their error-spotting: James Denney, Howard Silber, Bob Williams, Carl Keith, William Arendt and Irene Provost. Their knowledge of Nebraska runs deep—altogether more than three hundred years worth.

Among the present *Omaha World-Herald* staff members who gave me a hand in checking and verifying were Robert Tucker in sports and Jean Hauser, chief librarian. And there are other friends who fed me their favorite kernels of Nebraskianna when they learned about my project. I thank all of them.

I am also indebted to the Nebraska State Historical Society and the Historical Society of Douglas County for making their research facilities available to me. There is no dearth of valuable books on the history of Nebraska. I drew on several for facts which have long been imbedded in the chronicles of this state.

Any errors in the book—either of commission or of omission—are mine alone. Long after my deadline had past, I kept thinking of people, events, and data that should have been included.

My son, George, persuaded me to undertake the book and helped with the research. My wife, Maria Teresa, aided with the proofreading and provided much needed encouragement.

To all who so willingly assisted me in this project, I am grateful.

TABLE OF CONTENTS

GEOGRAPHY

C H A P T E R O N E

Q. Headquartered in Sidney, what company claims to be the largest and fastest growing mail-order sporting goods company in the world?

A. Cabela's.

Q. The site of what educational institution is known as "the Campus of a Thousand Oaks"?

A. Peru State College.

Q. Where is the new $18 million bridge across the Missouri River that will save eighty-five miles of travel between Nebraska and South Dakota?

A. Niobrara.

Q. How long is Nebraska from the Missouri River in the southeast to the Wyoming border in the northwest?

A. 459 miles.

Q. How much of the state's precipitation falls in the growing season?

A. Seven tenths.

Q. What is the lowest elevation in Nebraska?

A. 840 feet, near Falls City.

Q. Where is the highest point in the state, at 5,420 feet?

A. Near Kimball.

Q. What city is named after a 4,600 foot butte marking the Oregon and Mormon Trails?

A. Scottsbluff.

Q. What grass-covered area occupies about twenty thousand square miles in the northern portion of the state?

A. Sand Hills.

Q. How many varieties of native grass does Nebraska have?

A. Around 200, more than any other state.

Q. What pathway will eventually stretch 321 miles (over abandoned tracks) from Norfolk to Chadron?

A. Cowboy Trail.

Q. What dam, completed in 1941, created Lake McConaughy, the state's largest lake?

A. Kingsley.

Q. What town was named by the Union Pacific Railroad for a battlefield in Belgium?

A. Waterloo.

Q. What was the town of Pender called when it was two miles from its present location?

A. Athens.

Q. What Nebraska county is the largest in the United States and is bigger than Connecticut?

A. Cherry.

Q. How much of the state's rainfall is run-off?

A. One tenth.

Q. In what county is there a Beaver Crossing?

A. Seward.

Q. What Polk County community is known as "the Swedish capital of Nebraska"?

A. Stromsburg.

Q. What renowned strong man, son of a Frenchman and an Indian woman, had a town in southeast Nebraska named for him?

A. Antoine Barada.

Q. Charles Rouleau, a member of the Frémont expedition, gave his name to what town, with a change in spelling?

A. Rulo.

Q. What town was named after the Democratic candidate for president in 1876?

A. Tilden.

Q. Blue Boy, a world champion hog that went to Hollywood and appeared in the original *State Fair,* came from what town?

A. Pilger.

Q. President Calvin Coolidge visited what Nebraska town en route to the Pine Ridge Indian Reservation in South Dakota?

A. Rushville.

Q. What town was named for the home of Henry Clay, near Lexington, Kentucky?

A. Ashland.

Q. In what year did Omaha University, a municipal school, become the University of Nebraska at Omaha, a state school?

A. 1968.

Q. What town in southwest Nebraska had three names— Scratchpot, Pickleville, and Northwood—before its present one?

A. Cambridge.

Q. What city was named in honor of an ex-colonel associated with the Saint Joseph and Grand Island Railroad?

A. Hastings.

Q. Alliance originally had what name?

A. Grand Lake.

Q. What was the name of the fort on the Oregon Trail that later became Fort Kearny, the namesake for the town Kearney?

A. Fort Chiles.

Q. Who called the stretch of Highway 2 from Grand Island to Alliance one of the nation's twenty most spectacular roads?

A. Charles Kuralt.

Q. Where is the world-renowned Agate Fossil Beds National Monument?

A. South of Harrison.

Q. What historic site was once a breeding center for army horses and mules?

A. Fort Robinson.

Q. Who built the artifact-packed Pioneer Village in Minden?

A. Harold Warp.

Q. What is the highest waterfall in Nebraska?

A. Smith Falls (seventy feet).

Q. At what three sites did the air force place Blue Scout missiles to launch emergency communications satellites?

A. Tekamah, West Point, and Wisner.

Q. In what state park can rock carvings be found in a cave?

A. Indian Cave.

Q. In what Sand Hills county was this sign once posted: "Welcome to Ainsworth, the Middle of No Where"?

A. Brown.

Q. Where are the two largest units of the state Department of Correctional Services?

A. Lincoln and Omaha.

Q. What is the name of the four-story Victorian home that Williams Jennings Bryan built in Lincoln in 1902?

A. Fairview.

Q. Where is the multimillion dollar Benedictine mission house built by monks who fled Nazi Germany?

A. Schuyler.

Q. What town calls itself "the Best Town in Nebraska by a Dam Site"?

A. Fairbury.

Q. With twenty-two thousand residents, what is the largest population center in the Panhandle?

A. Scottsbluff/Gering.

Q. In what winter was a series of snowstorms so bad that hay was airlifted to cattle in the Sand Hills?

A. 1948–49.

Q. Where is Toadstool Park, a geologic treasure where circular sandstone slabs sit atop eroded stems of Brule clay?

A. Near Crawford.

Q. What is the nickname of the world's largest fossil elephant found near Wellfleet and displayed at the University of Nebraska?

A. Archie.

Q. What town was the northernmost point of the Santa Fe Railroad?

A. Superior.

Q. Who is the largest private employer in Nebraska?

A. Iowa Beef Packing.

Q. What is the leading type of manufacturing in Nebraska?

A. Food processing.

Q. Douglas County contains what percentage of the state's population?

A. Around 25 percent.

Q. What ethnic group provided the largest number of early settlers in Nebraska?

A. German.

Q. African-Americans made up what percentage of the state's population in 1990?

A. 3.6 percent.

Q. What was the median age of Nebraskans in 1990?

A. Thirty-three years old.

Q. What percentage of the population reported Hispanic origins in the 1990 census?

A. 2.3 percent.

Q. What percentage of Nebraskans was born in Nebraska, according to the 1990 census?

A. 70 percent.

Q. What was the only decade in which Nebraska lost population?

A. 1930-40.

Q. What building material is yielded by the Arikaree and Ogallala rocks?

A. Plaster.

Q. The Henry Doorly Zoo in Omaha was named for the publisher of what newspaper?

A. The *Omaha World-Herald*.

Q. What state park had the largest attendance in 1995?

A. Mahoney.

Q. When did the University of Nebraska at Kearney become part of the university system?

A. 1991.

Q. What four sovereign Nebraska Indian tribes have democratic forms of government?

A. Omaha, Ponca, Santee Sioux, and Winnebago.

Q. How many major airlines serve Omaha?

A. Twelve.

Q. Where is the geographical center of Nebraska?

A. In Custer County, ten miles northwest of Broken Bow.

Q. Not including Nebraska City with its Arbor Lodge, what town claims to have more varieties of trees than any other in Nebraska?

A. Bellwood.

Q. How did the century-old Omaha civic organization Ak-Sar-Ben get its name?

A. Nebraska spelled backwards.

Q. Where does Nebraska rank among the states in population?

A. Thirty-eighth.

Q. How many universities and colleges are in Omaha?

A. Nine.

Q. Where does the Kingsley Dam rank in size among U.S. embankment dams?

A. Eleventh.

Q. What popular Lincoln restaurant is named for William Jennings Bryan?

A. Billy's.

Q. What was the median price of existing family homes in Omaha in 1996?

A. $84,600.

———⊗⊗⊗———

Q. When were the Ak-Sar-Ben and South Omaha Bridges connecting Omaha with Council Bluffs freed from tolls?

A. September 25, 1947.

———⊗⊗⊗———

Q. Where is the annual Czech festival held the first week of August?

A. Wilber.

———⊗⊗⊗———

Q. What year was the great Missouri River flood when citizens of Omaha and Council Bluffs helped save their cities by sandbagging?

A. 1952.

———⊗⊗⊗———

Q. The annual Applejack Festival, which draws forty thousand people, is held in what town?

A. Nebraska City.

———⊗⊗⊗———

Q. What is the tallest building in Omaha at 30 stories and 469 feet?

A. Woodmen Tower.

———⊗⊗⊗———

Q. Of the twenty-five least populated counties in the United States, nine are in what region of Nebraska?

A. Sand Hills.

Q. What was the date of the big flood on the Republican River in which more than one hundred people lost their lives in one night?

A. June 1, 1935.

Q. What was the name given to today's Elkhorn River by the early French-Canadians?

A. *La Corne de Cerf* ("stag horn" in French).

Q. Annual flood damage along what river is the highest of any basin in the state?

A. Elkhorn.

Q. What is the name of Omaha's airport?

A. Eppley Airfield.

Q. Who gave the name *Its Kari Kitsu* ("plenty potatoes river") to the stream Nebraskans now call the Loup?

A. Pawnees.

Q. In what state do Nebraska's Big and Little Blue Rivers join?

A. Kansas.

Q. The family of U.S. Sen. Kenneth Wherry ran a mortuary in what town?

A. Pawnee City.

Q. When did commercial barge traffic on the Missouri River reach Omaha?

A. 1955.

Q. Where is the 269-foot dredge boat known as the *Meriwether Lewis* now kept in permanent dry dock?

A. Brownville.

Q. What are Nebraska's four most populous cities?

A. Omaha, Lincoln, Bellevue, and Grand Island.

Q. What city is the home of the famous Chicken Show held every July?

A. Wayne.

Q. What town claims to be "the Groundhog Capital of Nebraska"?

A. Unadilla.

Q. What is the name of the Iowa enclave created when the Missouri River cut a new channel at Omaha to form an oxbow lake?

A. Carter Lake.

Q. In 1962 who declared Wilber "the Czech capital of Nebraska"?

A. Gov. Frank Morrison.

Q. What was Omaha's ranking among U.S. cities in population in 1996?

A. Forty-fifth.

Q. What caused Lexington to grow more than 50 percent between 1990 and 1996?

A. Meat-packing.

Q. In 1996 what was Omaha's estimated population, a total that put it just behind Miami?

A. 364,253.

Q. Where is the only gambling casino in Nebraska?

A. Santee Sioux Reservation.

Q. The restaurant at Mahoney State Park offers entrees of what well-known prairie animal?

A. Buffalo.

Q. Where are the manuscripts and awards of author Bess Streeter Aldrich kept?

A. Elmwood Library.

Q. In what Lincoln district does the Midwest's largest farmers' market take place from May to October?

A. Haymarket.

Q. From how many miles away can the four hundred-foot state capitol be seen?

A. Thirty.

―――∞∞∞―――

Q. In what Lincoln park can one find four sandstone columns that were once part of the U.S. Treasury Building in Washington, D.C.?

A. Pioneers.

―――∞∞∞―――

Q. The restaurant where a German-Russian sandwich known as the *runza* was first sold is in what city?

A. Lincoln.

―――∞∞∞―――

Q. What is the name of the Lincoln turn-of-the-century warehouse district that now houses boutiques, art shops, and restaurants?

A. Haymarket.

―――∞∞∞―――

Q. What river runs through McCook?

A. Republican.

―――∞∞∞―――

Q. Lincoln claims to have the longest main street in the world because its principal thoroughfare, O Street, runs fifty miles straight east to what town?

A. Union.

―――∞∞∞―――

Q. In what town can the 24,490-pound rock that was at one time a marker on the Ox-Bow Trail be found?

A. Wahoo.

Q. In what town is the only covered bridge in Nebraska?

A. Cook (in Johnson County).

Q. What town in Nemaha County originally was called Podunk?

A. Brock.

Q. Where is the Heartland of America Park, with a fifteen-acre lake, three-hundred-foot lighted fountain, and summer concerts?

A. Omaha.

Q. Containing a stone chapel sometimes used for weddings, Coryell Park is in what town?

A. Auburn.

Q. Where is the 1881 Crackerbox Schoolhouse, said to be the smallest in the United States?

A. Pawnee City.

Q. What autumnal Omaha festival was conceived as a salute to labor?

A. Septemberfest.

Q. What state recreation area has ten railroad cabooses available for rent as cabins?

A. Two Rivers.

Q. Where is a collection of more than eight hundred kinds of barbed wire?

A. Pawnee City.

━━━◦≈≈◦━━━

Q. Prairies make up how much of the state's regions?

A. About three fourths.

━━━◦≈≈◦━━━

Q. Omaha's Gene Leahy Mall, with its lagoon, walking paths, and sculptures, took its name from the holder of what office?

A. Mayor.

━━━◦≈≈◦━━━

Q. Where can you find a display of memorabilia of actor Robert Taylor?

A. Beatrice.

━━━◦≈≈◦━━━

Q. What is Nebraska's official Fourth of July City?

A. Seward.

━━━◦≈≈◦━━━

Q. What area is the biggest producer of potatoes in Nebraska?

A. Panhandle.

━━━◦≈≈◦━━━

Q. What Omaha restaurant occupies the site of the Philadelphia Leather Company, which sold boots to George V of England and Gustav V of Sweden?

A. Old Chicago Brewery.

Q. Where do the North and South Platte Rivers join?

A. Near the city of North Platte.

Q. A touring coach used by President William Howard Taft and his family is housed in what building in Cozad?

A. 100th Meridian Museum.

Q. What author contributed fifty thousand dollars to help re-create a cattle ranch at a planned Nebraska National Trails Museum in the Brule-Ogallala area?

A. James A. Michener.

Q. Omaha's first indoor swimming pool was in the lower level of what building?

A. J. P. Cooke.

Q. In 1998 who bought the 44,744-acre Milligan Ranch south of Rushville, bringing his Sand Hills holdings to 96,513 acres?

A. Ted Turner.

Q. In what town is the Baled Hay Church (Pilgrim Holiness Church), which is built of hay and covered with plaster, located?

A. Arthur.

Q. What department store occupying the 1906 building at Sixteenth and Douglas Streets in Omaha boasted "Everything you want is at…"?

A. Brandeis.

Q. A humorous re-creation of England's ancient Stonehenge, built of old cars by Jim Reinders near Alliance, has what name?

A. Carhenge.

Q. What is the second largest lake within Nebraska?

A. Harlan County Reservoir.

Q. What was the first paved transcontinental highway whose Nebraska segment was completed in 1915?

A. Lincoln Highway (Route 30).

Q. What Omaha hotel at Fourteenth and Farnam Streets burned in 1878, killing five firemen?

A. Grand Central.

Q. How many Native Americans live in Nebraska?

A. Approximately 12,400.

Q. In what counties are Nebraska's salt marshes, with their unique and declining community of salt-loving plants?

A. Lancaster and Saunders.

Q. What fifty-employee company in Beatrice is Nebraska's largest producer of fruitcakes?

A. Grandma's Bake Shoppe.

Q. Where is one of the world's largest centers for Afghan studies?

A. University of Nebraska at Omaha.

Q. The city of Norfolk got its name because it is on the north fork of what river?

A. Elkhorn.

Q. The name of what town comes from an Indian word for a species of elm tree?

A. Wahoo.

Q. The Oregon Trail landmark Chimney Rock was noted and described by what percent of the trail's travelers in their diaries?

A. Ninety-five.

Q. What was the name of the Omaha judge in the Standing Bear trial whose name was given to a Nebraska county?

A. Elmer Dundy.

Q. What town in Webster County was originally called "In a Valley," but the name was shortened by the post office?

A. Inavale.

Q. What is the difference in elevation between the eastern and western parts of the state?

A. 4,580 feet.

Q. Where is the only Oregon Trail Park in Nebraska?

A. The village of Oak.

Q. What Nebraska town claims it is "the Popcorn Capital" of the state?

A. North Bend.

Q. When did the Bucholz Well, west of Falls City, officially become Nebraska's first producing oil well?

A. July 27, 1940.

Q. What structure in Nebraska City is the state's oldest public building still in use?

A. Otoe County Courthouse.

Q. Where was the nation's first off-premise banking developed, with teller machines at grocery store courtesy counters?

A. Lincoln.

Q. In what county was there a 656 foot-deep well yielding, for a time, 2,500 gallons per minute at 95 pounds of pressure?

A. Knox County, in 1896.

Q. Where is "the world's largest porch swing" whose users claim can seat twenty-five adults?

A. Hebron.

Q. In what town is a torpedo displayed in memory of the USS *Wahoo,* a submarine sunk by the Japanese in 1943 after it destroyed twenty ships?

A. Wahoo.

———∞∞∞———

Q. What former military installation near Ord has been restored to its original 1870s condition?

A. Fort Hartsuff.

———∞∞∞———

Q. Boys Town moved to what 160-acre farm eleven miles west of Omaha in 1921?

A. Overlook Farm.

———∞∞∞———

Q. What town stages Popcorn Days every August?

A. North Loup.

———∞∞∞———

Q. "The World's Largest Kolache Festival" takes place in what town?

A. Prague.

———∞∞∞———

Q. What town is situated at the intersection of Interstate 80 and the 100th Meridian?

A. Cozad.

———∞∞∞———

Q. What is the largest lake between the Great Lakes and Great Salt Lake?

A. Lake McConaughy.

Q. What do these three cities have in common: Shizuoka, Japan; Braunschweig, Germany; and Siauliai, Lithuania?

A. All Sister Cities of Omaha.

Q. When did Buffalo Bill stage the nation's first rodeo in North Platte?

A. July 4, 1882.

Q. Because of its wild western ways, what Nebraska town was once known as "the Gomorrah of the Plains"?

A. Ogallala.

Q. Where is the intersection of Interstate 80 and U.S. 81, two highways that run border to border?

A. York.

Q. How many lakes are in Nebraska?

A. About 2,500.

Q. What causes the large green circles on the land that air travelers spot in rural Nebraska?

A. Center pivot irrigation.

Q. Each Christmas season where can Omahans view dozens of objects made of gingerbread?

A. Mormon Cemetery Visitors Center.

Q. What are the Platte River's principal tributaries?

A. Loup and Elkhorn.

―――∞∞∞―――

Q. What river drains the northern border of Nebraska?

A. Niobrara.

―――∞∞∞―――

Q. John Brown's Cave, one of the stations of the Underground Railroad for slaves escaping from the South, is in what city?

A. Nebraska City.

―――∞∞∞―――

Q. After the Firehouse Dinner Theater closed, what restaurant moved into one of Omaha's oldest fire barns?

A. Upstream Brewing Company.

―――∞∞∞―――

Q. What is the area of Nebraska?

A. 77,355 square miles.

―――∞∞∞―――

Q. Where does Nebraska rank among the states in area?

A. Fifteenth.

―――∞∞∞―――

Q. What was the population of Nebraska in the 1990 census?

A. 1,578,385.

Q. By what percentage did Nebraska's birthrate drop between 1980 and 1990?

A. 10.9 percent.

Q. How many states border Nebraska?

A. Six.

Q. When did the Union Pacific construct its bridge across the Missouri River between Omaha and Council Bluffs?

A. 1872.

Q. What river runs through Beatrice?

A. Big Blue.

Q. What Nebraska post office always expects a marked increase in its mail early in February?

A. Valentine.

Q. Where is Dana College?

A. Blair.

Q. What Panhandle town is well known because of a sandwich named for it?

A. McGrew (McGrewburger).

Q. Where is the nation's only church that has reversible pews, and a Protestant altar at one end and a Catholic one at the other?

A. Keystone.

Q. How much of Nebraska's 77,358 square miles is inland water?

A. 481.

Q. What Chinese restaurant has been in operation in downtown Omaha since 1920?

A. King Fong Cafe.

Q. Known previously as Salt Lake and Burlington Beach, what is the body of water at Lincoln now called?

A. Capitol Beach.

Q. With 147,000 members, what is the largest religious denomination in the Omaha metropolitan area?

A. Roman Catholic.

Q. What bank built a futuristic building in downtown Omaha that was nicknamed "the Cupcake" because of its shape?

A. Omaha National Bank.

Q. In what part of Omaha does a self-guided walking tour go past the oldest mill and oldest bank in Nebraska?

A. Florence.

Q. What Czech restaurant in Omaha has a singing commercial that starts, "Dumplings and kraut today…"?

A. Bohemian Cafe.

Q. In Lincoln, the thirty-eight-foot-tall concrete Cascade Fountain is dedicated to whom?

A. The state's retired teachers.

Q. Civil War general Nelson Miles lived long enough to participate in an Omaha parade in what year?

A. 1925.

Q. Scotts Bluff National Monument was named for what fur trader who died near the site in 1828?

A. Hiram Scott.

Q. What Omaha jewelry store owned by Warren Buffett sold an engagement ring to Bill Gates?

A. Borsheim's.

Q. From what town did prospectors head north to the Black Hills gold rush?

A. Sidney.

Q. Because of its large number of houses of worship, what town has been called "Church City"?

A. Lincoln.

Q. What town calls itself "the Alfalfa Capital"?

A. Cozad.

Q. Where is the world's largest American Legion post?

A. Lincoln.

Q. What river was described by early explorers as "one mile wide and one inch deep"?

A. Platte.

Q. How many other state capitols are built in the same "skyscraper" style as Nebraska's?

A. Three (North Dakota, Louisiana, and Florida).

Q. How many cities in Nebraska have populations of more than ten thousand?

A. Thirteen.

Q. What is Nebraska's oldest state park?

A. Chadron.

Q. What Sand Hills rancher donated her Bar 99 Ranch to the Game and Parks Commission so it could function as a living history museum?

A. Eva Bowring.

Q. When was the first highway from Omaha to Kansas City completed?

A. 1911.

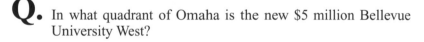

Q. Where is the Tower of Four Winds, a forty-five-foot tall rock structure representing a vision by Black Elk?

A. Blair.

Q. Charles Starkweather, the murderer of eleven people in 1958, is buried where?

A. Wyuka Cemetery, Lincoln.

Q. What businessman paid for construction of the Gerald R. Ford Birthsite and Gardens in Omaha?

A. James Paxson.

Q. In what quadrant of Omaha is the new $5 million Bellevue University West?

A. Northwest.

Q. What was the name of the sandwich invented at Omaha's Blackstone Hotel that consists of rye bread, corned beef, Swiss cheese, and sauerkraut?

A. Reuben.

Q. What Missouri River town once boasted several cigar factories?

A. Plattsmouth.

Q. What town was the site of a mini gold rush in 1907 that proved to be fruitless?

A. Wymore.

Q. About seven hundred refugees from what east African country have settled in Omaha?

A. Sudan.

Q. What privately-owned Omaha construction company, among the world's largest, has expanded into an empire of coal mining, communications, and electronics enterprises?

A. Peter Kiewit Sons' Inc.

Q. What Nebraska building so impressed Franklin D. Roosevelt that he ordered the Bethesda Naval Hospital designed in the same style?

A. The state capitol.

Q. How many meandering miles of the Missouri River skirts the eastern boarder?

A. Five hundred.

Q. When did barge traffic on the Missouri River peak at 3.3 million tons per year?

A. In the late 1970s.

Q. Where is the Stolley Recreation Area that has groves of more than fifty varieties of trees?

A. Grand Island.

Q. What native of Fairbury is the vice commander of the U.S. Strategic Command at Omaha's Offutt Air Force Base?

A. Adm. Dennis Jones.

Q. What civil engineer for whom a college at Crete was named built the Burlington & Missouri River Railroad across Nebraska?

A. Thomas Doane.

Q. With approximately two hundred students enrolled, what Far Eastern country dominates the foreign population at Bellevue University?

A. Nepal.

Q. Where are the world's first test-tube tigers raised?

A. Henry Doorly Zoo in Omaha.

Q. What is the nation's largest farm management firm which runs five thousand farms in twenty-two states from its Omaha headquarters?

A. Farmers National Co.

Q. What marks the well in Aurora that prior to settlement was a popular resting spot on the Nebraska City cutoff of the Oregon Trail?

A. Deepwell Ranch Monument.

Q. What building occupies the structure that housed the tiny Brownville Medical College created by the Territorial Legislature in 1857?

A. Brownville Methodist Church.

Q. What is Nebraska's top cash crop?

A. Corn.

Q. What county do the Mormon Pioneer, the Nebraska City Cutoff, the Oregon, the Ox Bow, and the Pony Express Trails all pass through?

A. Hall.

Q. Where can one find a sculpture of a horse and rider made out of miles of barbed wire?

A. Sod House Museum, in Gothenburg.

Q. What two railroads haul most of the coal that is mined in Wyoming across Nebraska to eastern and southern markets?

A. Union Pacific and Burlington Northern Santa Fe.

Q. What town claims to have the last functional water-powered flour mill in the state?

A. Champion.

Q. Overlooking the North Platte River, what five hundred-foot landmark marked the end of the prairies to pioneers heading west?

A. Chimney Rock.

Q. Pawnee Park, in Columbus, contains what structure that honors Christopher Columbus's first voyage to the New World?

A. The Quincentenary Belltower.

ENTERTAINMENT

C H A P T E R   T W O

Q. Which founding member of the Eagles rock group was born in Scottsbluff?

A. Randy Meisner.

Q. What town was made the new "home office" of David Letterman's *Late Show* in May 1996?

A. Wahoo.

Q. What Omaha resident is the musical artist behind Mannheim Steamroller?

A. Chip Davis.

Q. Tecumseh was the location for the filming of what 1980s television miniseries?

A. *Amerika.*

Q. What 1991 film directed by Sean Penn was partly filmed in Plattsmouth?

A. *The Indian Runner.*

Q. The movie *To Wong Foo, Thanks for Everything, Julie Newmar* starring Patrick Swayze, Wesley Snipes, and John Leguizamo was filmed on location in what tiny Nebraska town?

A. Loma.

Q. What year did Spencer Tracy win the Academy Award for Best Actor for his portrayal of Father Flanagan in *Boys Town*?

A. 1938.

Q. The king and queen crowned at the Ak-Sar-Ben Coronation Ball in Omaha reign over what mythical kingdom?

A. Quivira.

Q. Wahoo is the hometown of what co-founder of Twentieth-Century Fox and winner of seven Academy Awards?

A. Darryl Zanuck.

Q. What movie dancing star, whose real name was Austerlitz, was born on Omaha's South Tenth Street?

A. Fred Astaire.

Q. What singer's album *Nebraska* has a song based on the shooting spree of Charles Starkweather?

A. Bruce Springsteen.

Q. Where was Hollywood actor James Coburn born?

A. Laurel.

Q. What was the name of the movie in which footballer Gale Sayers of Omaha was depicted as one of the leading characters?

A. *Brian's Song.*

Q. What Omahan directed the 1995 movie *Citizen Ruth* starring Laura Dern?

A. Alexander Payne.

Q. What Academy Award-winning actor was born in Grand Island and grew up in Omaha?

A. Henry Fonda.

Q. Television star Johnny Carson was born in Corning, Iowa, but in what Nebraska town was he raised?

A. Norfolk.

Q. Along with his sister Adele, what native Omahan danced with a vaudeville troupe in Omaha in 1908?

A. Fred Astaire.

Q. What star of *The Godfather* lived in Omaha during his early childhood?

A. Marlon Brando.

Q. What movie star attended two Omaha high schools—Benson and Westside—plus the University of Nebraska at Omaha?

A. Nick Nolte.

Q. What star of the film *Raintree County* was born in Omaha in 1920 with his twin sister, Roberta?

A. Montgomery Clift.

Q. Born in Omaha, what Tony Award-winning actress starred in the television series *Sisters*?

A. Swoosie Kurtz.

Q. Born in Filley, what major movie actor attended high school in Beatrice?

A. Robert Taylor.

Q. What bespectacled silent film comedian and director was born in Burchard?

A. Harold Lloyd.

Q. Who made her stage debut at the Omaha Community Playhouse in 1930 and went on to become a major movie star?

A. Dorothy McGuire.

Q. What early star of cowboy films was born in Tekamah?

A. Edmund "Hoot" Gibson.

Q. Ward Bond, whose credits range from early westerns to *Gone With the Wind* to *Wagon Train,* was born in what town?

A. Benkelman.

Q. What television celebrity host attended Lincoln High School?

A. Dick Cavett.

Q. What Academy Award-winner for her role in *Who's Afraid of Virginia Woolf* attended Lincoln High School one year behind Dick Cavett?

A. Sandy Dennis.

Q. Rodney Grant, who had a feature role in *Dances with Wolves,* grew up in what town?

A. Macy.

Q. Born and raised in Brainard, what character actor graduated from Omaha Commerce High School in the 1920s?

A. Lyle Talbot.

Q. What annual Omaha western show, founded in 1947, has featured such performers as Fibber McGee and Molly, Harpo Marx, Roy Rogers, and Dale Evans?

A. Ak-Sar-Ben Champion Rodeo.

Q. When Omaha's refurbished Orpheum Theater reopened in 1975 who was the headliner?

A. Red Skelton.

Q. What torch singer of the 1920s and 1930s, who helped to popularize the songs "Shine On Harvest Moon" and "Ten Cents a Dance," was raised in David City?

A. Ruth Etting.

Q. What Nebraska high school was the principal location for the 1998 movie *Election* starring Matthew Broderick?

A. Papillion-LaVista.

Q. In 1991 what noted singer rented a home north of Omaha to record his *Different Directions* album?

A. John Denver.

Q. What son of a famous actor starred in Omaha Community Playhouse and Omaha University productions in the 1950s?

A. Peter Fonda.

Q. What was Nebraska-born actor Robert Taylor's real name?

A. Spangler Arlington Brugh.

Q. What stars of *Strategic Air Command* attended its world premiere in Omaha's Orpheum Theater in the early 1950s?

A. Jimmy Stewart and June Allyson.

Q. The role of William Jennings Bryan in *Inherit the Wind,* a movie about the Scopes trial, was played by what actor?

A. Fredric March.

Q. What graduate of Omaha's Creighton Prep plays the part of David Allen in the soap opera *As the World Turns*?

A. Danny Markel.

Q. What retired schoolteacher has played the role of Scrooge in the Omaha Community Theater's *Christmas Carol* for twenty-two years?

A. Dick Boyd.

Q. Duke Ellington, Count Basie, and Louis Armstrong once performed at what ballroom on Omaha's North Twenty-fourth Street?

A. Dreamland Hall.

Q. In 1997 what former star of television's *Good Times* joined the staff of Omaha's KKAR?

A. Jimmie "J. J." Walker.

Q. What Nebraskan served as Gen. Dwight Eisenhower's press officer and later became "King of Hollywood Press Agents"?

A. Barney Oldfield.

Q. Who wrote the song "Omaha" in 1922 for an Ak-Sar-Ben membership drive?

A. Fritz "Al" Carlson.

Q. What mother of a famous actor starred in the Omaha Community Theater production *The Enchanted Cottage* in 1924?

A. Dorothy Brando.

Q. In 1989 where in Europe did the Omaha Community Playhouse present *Quilters*?

A. Soviet Union.

Q. What Nebraska professional theatrical touring company appears across the nation and in Canada?

A. Nebraska Theatre Caravan.

—— ❦ ——

Q. How many playgoers attend the performances of the Omaha Community Theater each year?

A. Around 125,000.

—— ❦ ——

Q. During the summer where in Omaha do jazz lovers congregate on Thursdays for food, drink, and concerts?

A. Joslyn's Jazz on the Green.

—— ❦ ——

Q. What is the name of the Sunday morning classical music program at Joslyn Art Museum that features a light brunch?

A. Bagels and Bach.

—— ❦ ——

Q. Where do audiences on blankets and lawn chairs watch free "Shakespeare on the Green" performances every summer?

A. University of Nebraska at Omaha.

—— ❦ ——

Q. Where is the three-day Summer Arts Festival held?

A. Downtown Omaha.

—— ❦ ——

Q. According to the Greater Omaha Chamber of Commerce, how much money was spent on Omaha's arts and entertainment in the past five years?

A. Around $200 million.

Q. Where is Omaha's annual Dickens Christmas celebration of song and dance held?

A. Old Market.

———

Q. What city's ballet company is a partner with Ballet Omaha in presenting three productions each year, including *The Nutcracker*?

A. Dayton, Ohio.

———

Q. Funded by local businesses, what organization distributes $1.6 million each year to support Omaha arts groups?

A. United Arts Omaha.

———

Q. What Omaha church holds a midwinter Flower Festival that draws more than ten thousand visitors?

A. Saint Cecilia's Cathedral.

———

Q. How many men bowlers compete in the Greater Omaha Bowling Association?

A. Ten thousand.

———

Q. Who created the opera *Requiem,* which had its world premiere in Omaha?

A. Andrew Lloyd Webber.

———

Q. How many theaters did downtown Omaha have in 1863?

A. Seven.

Q. What actress/author chose the Omaha Community Playhouse to premiere her original play about Marilyn Monroe?

A. Katie LaBourdette.

Q. Who prepared an exhibit for the Joslyn Art Museum after being inspired by the plaster cast of a little dancer?

A. Richard Kendall, a renowned Degas scholar.

Q. Where does the Omaha Theater for Young People rank nationally in percentage of population that attends its theater?

A. First.

Q. What musical organization scheduled appearances by Itzhak Perlman, Marvin Hamlisch, Steve Lawrence, and Eydie Gorme in its 1997–98 season?

A. Omaha Symphony.

Q. The first phase of a $22 million renovation was completed by what Omaha museum in 1996?

A. Durham Western Heritage Museum.

Q. Where was a flamboyant production of the opera *Aida* staged in which an elephant in the cast broke loose?

A. Omaha's Ak-Sar-Ben Coliseum.

Q. What Nebraska city claims to offer more park acres per capita than any other U.S. city?

A. Lincoln.

Q. What is the most heavily used state recreational area, with about eight hundred thousand visits annually?

A. Branched Oak.

———

Q. Although big band leader Glenn Miller was born in Clarinda, Iowa, he lived for a longer time in what two Nebraska towns?

A. Tryon and North Platte.

———

Q. The movie *Badlands,* with Martin Sheen and Sissy Spacek, is based on what events in the Lincoln area?

A. The Starkweather shootings.

———

Q. Where is the converted hog barn, now called the Loft Theater, where the Born-in-a-Barn Players have produced plays for twenty years?

A. Weeping Water.

———

Q. Who has been chairman of Godfather's Pizza, president of the National Restaurant Association, and a singer who has soloed with the Omaha Symphony?

A. Herman Cain.

———

Q. What Omaha jazz musician toured with Count Basie for several years in the mid-1940s?

A. Preston Love.

———

Q. What former professional football running back who once lived in Omaha is co-star of the television show *Mortal Kombat: Annihilation?*

A. Lynn "Red" Williams.

Q. What Omaha journalism organization has been lampooning Nebraska political figures at its annual ball for half a century?

A. Omaha Press Club.

Q. Where does Omaha's only professional cabaret troupe stage performances and organize regional tours?

A. Dundee Dinner Theater.

Q. What theatrical group presents melodramas each spring during Florence Days?

A. Florentine Players.

Q. Who is the director of the fifty-five-member Sweet Adelines Omaha Chorus?

A. Judy Aden.

Q. What two hundred-member community chorus directed by Greg Zielke performs Handel's *Messiah* each holiday season?

A. Voices of Omaha.

Q. Josie Metal-Corbin directs what dance troupe at the University of Nebraska at Omaha?

A. The Moving Company.

Q. What concert band, with eighty to ninety members, performs all year long in eastern Nebraska?

A. Nebraska Wind Symphony.

Q. What is the last name of the Omaha sisters—Heather, Jamie, Rachel, and Allison—who form the Mulberry Lane singing group?

A. Rizzuto.

———∞———

Q. What entertainer has been making a name for herself in Omaha by playing the dulcimer?

A. Phyllis Dunne.

———∞———

Q. Where was rock musician Matthew Sweet born?

A. Lincoln.

———∞———

Q. Who is the Omaha folk singer and composer whose *River City Folk* public radio broadcasts are heard across the nation each week?

A. Tom May.

———∞———

Q. When the train carrying the *Mr. Roberts* scenery to Omaha was stuck in an Iowa blizzard in 1951, what famous actor performed with fellow cast members on a bare stage?

A. Henry Fonda.

———∞———

Q. What native Omahan has been casting director for more than four hundred feature films and television shows?

A. Lynn Stalmaster.

———∞———

Q. Thuri Ravenscroft of Norfolk is the voice of what salesman for Kellogg's Sugar Frosted Flakes?

A. Tony the Tiger.

Q. What Omaha Benson High School student, named Miss Victory at a school ball, became an internationally known chanteuse?

A. Julie Wilson.

Q. What former Omaha District 66 teacher was one of the four Navarro Sisters who sang with the Wayne King and Phil Spitalny bands?

A. Mrs. Reid (Mercedes) Cameron.

Q. Omahans Nick Hexum, Chad Sexton, Tim Mahoney, Aaron Wills, and Doug Martinez form what popular musical group?

A. 311.

Q. When did the multitalented Lyle DeMoss, raconteur, culinary expert, singer, actor, and announcer with WOW and KFAB, break into Nebraska radio?

A. 1926, at York.

Q. After the community raised $16 million for renovations, what museum recently added a wing and seven galleries?

A. Omaha's Joslyn Art Museum.

Q. Who was in the announcer's booth in 1949 when WOW-TV became the first television station to sign on in Omaha?

A. Johnny Carson.

Q. Who was the portly announcer of the *Jack Benny Show* born in Lincoln?

A. Don Wilson.

Q. What composer/singer, who was a native of Omaha, composed "We've Only Just Begun" and "An Old-Fashioned Love Song"?

A. Paul Williams.

———∞∞———

Q. What Lincoln actor was a regular performer on television's *Charlie's Angels*?

A. David Doyle.

———∞∞———

Q. Where was actor David Janssen, who starred in *The Fugitive*, born?

A. Naponee.

———∞∞———

Q. What singing star of *Oklahoma* and *Carousel* lived in Lincoln during the latter years of his life?

A. Gordon MacRae.

———∞∞———

Q. George Raymond Wagner, a professional wrestler born in Seward, took what show business name?

A. Gorgeous George.

———∞∞———

Q. What Hollywood actor from Hildreth performed in westerns for thirty years and was known as "the Movie Bad Man"?

A. Pierce Lyden.

———∞∞———

Q. Where did Robert Hays, star of the movie *Airplane!*, attend high school?

A. Bellevue.

Q. What Omaha actress was a regular on the television series *Benson*?

A. Inga Swenson.

Q. In what film did Damian O'Flynn of Omaha have a featured part?

A. *Wake Island.*

Q. What is the hometown of Skip Stephenson, star of television's *Real People*?

A. Omaha.

Q. Roy Barcroft, western film performer, came from what town?

A. Crab Orchard.

Q. Lincoln actor William Fawcett was featured in what television series?

A. *Fury.*

Q. What singer/actress from Omaha and York sang "Thanks for the Memory" with Bob Hope in *The Big Broadcast of 1937*?

A. Shirley Ross.

Q. What former Omahan produced the television series *Batman* and was married to actress Joan Fontaine and later to actress Ann Rutherford?

A. Bill Dozier.

Q. George "Buddy" Miles, drummer, singer, and songwriter, attended what high school?

A. Omaha North.

––––––∞––––––

Q. Who was the musical arranger and composer with dozens of movie credits who moved to Omaha from Hastings?

A. Neal Hefti.

––––––∞––––––

Q. What president of the Omaha Central student council, circa 1913, became a movie matinee idol in the Roaring Twenties?

A. Rod la Rocque.

––––––∞––––––

Q. What native of Pawnee City, who attended Omaha Central High School, starred in the television series *Sheena, Queen of the Jungle*?

A. Irish McCalla.

––––––∞––––––

Q. During Gothenburg's Harvest Festival, what competition harks back to pioneer farming methods?

A. State Hand Cornhusking Contest.

––––––∞––––––

Q. Lorraine Gettman was the birth name of what Hollywood actress who was born in Lincoln, attended Omaha Central High School, and won a big role in *Cover Girl*?

A. Leslie Brooks.

––––––∞––––––

Q. What king of show business got his start doing card and magic tricks at Norfolk High School parties?

A. Johnny Carson.

Q. What actress's résumé includes Duchesne College, the Omaha Community Playhouse, and second billing, after Joan Bennett, in *Woman on the Beach*?

A. Virginia Huston.

Q. Born in Staplehurst, what movie actress played in *Red River* and *Kiss of Death*?

A. Coleen Gray.

Q. What graduate of Omaha's Westside High starred in *Weekend at Bernie's* and had character parts in some fifty plays on and off Broadway?

A. Terry Kiser.

Q. Who was the former Omaha auto dealer who gave millions of dollars to cultural activities, including a center for performing arts in Lincoln?

A. Ernest Lied.

Q. Who was the actor/singer/editor from Columbus and Omaha Central High School who founded, and for several years operated, Omaha's Firehouse Dinner Theater?

A. Dick Mueller.

Q. What Irish tenor on the *Lawrence Welk Show* comes from Grand Island?

A. Joe Feeney.

Q. What Omahan won an Oscar in 1996 for editing the Ron Howard film *Apollo 13*?

A. Mike Hill.

Q. As a teen, what television comedian from Burke High School performed magic tricks in Omaha's Old Market?

A. Pat Hazel.

Q. James Moeser, chancellor of the University of Nebraska, once was the official campus organist at what midwestern school?

A. University of Kansas.

Q. What South Dakotan was hired by Omaha KMTV's news director Mark Gautier as a reporter/photographer and a few years later became a network anchorman?

A. Tom Brokaw.

Q. What folklorist and television celebrity founded the National Liar's Hall of Fame in Dannebrog?

A. Roger Welsch.

Q. In 1997 what company closed eight movie theaters at one Omaha shopping mall and opened twenty-four at another mall five miles away?

A. AMC Entertainment, Incorporated.

Q. What Norfolk radio personality was elected to Congress largely because of his popular news program?

A. Karl Stefan.

Q. Some of the filming for *Terms of Endearment* took place in what city?

A. Lincoln.

Q. What television newsman from Omaha Benson High School became a Chicago and network anchorman?

A. Floyd Kalber.

Q. At the turn of the century, the Campbell Brothers Circus headquartered in what town?

A. Fairbury.

Q. What Omaha radio and television personality ended his broadcasts with the observation, "My time is up; thank you for yours"?

A. Merrill Workhoven.

Q. In 1993 the Counting Crows released what song with a Nebraska city as its title?

A. "Omaha."

Q. What announcer from television's *Laugh In* once worked at a radio station in Omaha?

A. Gary Owens.

Q. What award did Harold "Doc" Edgerton of Fremont and Aurora win for his 1940 film *Quicker 'n a Wink*?

A. An Oscar.

Q. The native Omaha actress, Swoosie Kurtz, is a cousin of which famous financier?

A. Warren Buffett.

Q. When Tommy Watkins of Cambridge assembled a band in Denver to tour the western states, who was one of his trombone players?

A. Glenn Miller.

Q. What director and producer with Pathé and RKO came from Ord?

A. Clyde E. Elliott.

Q. The autobiography of what Omaha musician has been published by Wesleyan University Press?

A. Preston Love.

Q. What radio singer from Lincoln also appeared in movies in the 1940s and 1950s?

A. Lucille Norman.

Q. What was the hometown of Wynonie Harris, rhythm and blues artist?

A. Omaha.

Q. What former Omahan directed several movies, including *Hester Street*?

A. Joan Micklin Silver.

Q. What jazz trumpeter came from Falls City?

A. PeeWee Erwin.

Q. What was the hometown of Rick Evans, of Zager & Evans, who recorded "In the Year 2525," a best-seller in 1969?

A. Lincoln.

Q. What rockabilly singer of the 1950s came from Omaha?

A. Sparkle Moore.

Q. In *Birth of a Nation* Abraham Lincoln was played by what actor/director from Omaha?

A. Joseph Henabery.

Q. What Nebraska-born actress appeared in *Lost in Yonkers* with Richard Dreyfuss and in *King Lear* with Paul Scofield?

A. Irene Worth.

Q. What child actor from Blair appeared in *Knute Rockne*?

A. Billy Dawson.

Q. What silent film comedian, who lived in Council Bluffs but once was an Omaha newsboy, played in *Hallelujah, I'm a Bum* with Al Jolson?

A. Harry Langdon.

Q. What popular Omaha bandleader became a stockbroker after hanging up his baton?

A. Lee Williams.

Q. What was the name of the singing group from Cambridge (Lloyd, Loyal, Wayne, and Detta) who were popular on radio in the Midwest during the 1920s?

A. The Decker Hawaiians.

Q. *Backpacker* magazine named what Nebraska stream one of the ten top canoeing rivers in the nation?

A. Niobrara.

Q. What lake with one hundred miles of white beaches draws boaters, windsurfers, anglers, and scuba divers?

A. McConaughy.

Q. What two Italian celebrations are held each summer in Omaha?

A. La Festa Italiana and Santa Lucia Festival.

Q. The mother of what actor gave Henry Fonda acting lessons in Omaha?

A. Marlon Brando.

Q. What school produces an eight-week summer repertory theater in Brownville?

A. Nebraska Wesleyan University.

Q. What is the terminus of the dinner train that originates in Fremont?

A. Hooper.

Q. What Mexican holiday is celebrated in South Omaha on or near May 5 each year?

A. Cinco de Mayo.

———⌘———

Q. Annually, how many visits are made to Lewis and Clark Lake on the Missouri River between Nebraska and South Dakota?

A. Around 2.5 million.

———⌘———

Q. When was the first powwow held at Macy by the Omaha Indians?

A. 1804.

———⌘———

Q. Where is the Little Britches Rodeo held for young riders every June?

A. Wymore.

———⌘———

Q. What town holds one of the largest Swedish celebrations in the nation each summer?

A. Oakland.

———⌘———

Q. What inventor created a fireworks museum in Norfolk?

A. Orville Henry Carlisle.

———⌘———

Q. Residents of what town celebrate Nebraska's Big Rodeo and Parade in late July each year?

A. Burwell.

Q. The Nebraska State Fair is held in Lincoln the first week of what month?

A. September.

———∞∞∞———

Q. What bandleader presided for years over the orchestra at Omaha's Paxton Hotel?

A. Paul Morehead.

———∞∞∞———

Q. What former centerpiece of recreation in Omaha featured big bands, a swimming pool, and kiddie rides?

A. Peony Park.

———∞∞∞———

Q. South Sioux City, Nebraska, and Sioux City, Iowa, join in what celebration on both sides of the Missouri River each June?

A. Siouxland Waterfest Weekend.

———∞∞∞———

Q. Where is the annual Douglas County Fair held?

A. Ak-Sar-Ben.

———∞∞∞———

Q. Where is Omaha constructing a new tennis center with space to eventually handle twenty-five courts?

A. Tranquility Park.

———∞∞∞———

Q. What Nebraska insurance company sponsored the national television show *Wild Kingdom*?

A. Mutual of Omaha.

Q. With balloon races, wild west show, and Civil War battles, where is the annual John C. Frémont Days celebration held?

A. Fremont.

Q. Opera Omaha commissioned composer Libby Larsen to write an opera, *Eric Hermannson's Soul,* adapted from a short story by what Nebraska author?

A. Willa Cather.

Q. What Nebraska high school won the 1997 National Cheerleading Association championship?

A. Papillion-LaVista.

Q. The Eagle Speedway and the I-80 Speedway are in what county?

A. Cass.

Q. The Kountze Memorial Theatre provides year-round dramatic productions at what state park?

A. Mahoney.

Q. Ice-skating is offered at what Omaha city parks?

A. Benson, Hitchcock, and Tranquility.

Q. With thousands of men growing beards for the occasion, when was the world premiere of the movie *Union Pacific* held in Omaha?

A. 1939.

Q. Who played a starring role as an ornery orphan in the movie *Boys Town*?

A. Mickey Rooney.

———∞∞∞———

Q. What 1955 movie was based on the life of David City's Ruth Etting, starring Doris Day and Jimmy Cagney?

A. *Love Me or Leave Me.*

———∞∞∞———

Q. What native Omahan played bass for Duke Ellington?

A. Alvin "Junior" Raglin.

———∞∞∞———

Q. What Omaha actor co-starred in Robert Duvall's *The Apostle*?

A. John Beasley.

———∞∞∞———

Q. For years what neighborhood Omaha theater showed *The Rocky Horror Picture Show* at midnight on Fridays and Saturday?

A. Admiral.

———∞∞∞———

Q. In 1987 what world-famous tenor canceled a concert in Omaha because of laryngitis but returned two and a half years later to make it up?

A. Plácido Domingo.

———∞∞∞———

Q. What comedienne was "nominated" for president in 1940 by the Surprise Party at a mock convention in Omaha's Ak-Sar-Ben Coliseum attended by six thousand "delegates"?

A. Gracie Allen.

Q. In the early days of WOW-TV in Omaha, who emceed such short-lived shows as *The Squirrel's Nest* and *Uncle Ank and Andy*?

A. Johnny Carson.

Q. For whom was Omaha's Rosenblatt Stadium named?

A. Mayor Johnny Rosenblatt.

Q. Where is Nebraska's first public skateboard park?

A. North Platte.

Q. What Cherry County town calls itself "the Canoe Capital of Nebraska"?

A. Sparks.

Q. What popular picnic and campus pastime was first tried in Lincoln?

A. Frisbee.

Q. What entertainment impresario has brought travelogues to Omaha's Joslyn Art Museum for forty-one seasons?

A. Dick Walter.

Q. What Nebraska racetrack is the first to open each year?

A. Fonner Park (in February).

Q. What former Associated Press reporter in Omaha became a syndicated columnist and participant in political talk shows?

A. Robert Novak.

———∞———

Q. In 1949 the first football game televised from Lincoln's Memorial Stadium was announced by what president-to-be of the Coca-Cola Company?

A. Don Keough.

———∞———

Q. What well-known band leader tried unsuccessfully to raise chickens in Omaha?

A. Lawrence Welk.

———∞———

Q. Where was the nation's first radio monitoring installation, built in 1930 to make sure each station stayed on the wave length assigned to it?

A. Grand Island.

———∞———

Q. What singer who was raised in Royal was a popular recording star in New York during the 1960s and 1970s?

A. Jeri Southern.

———∞———

Q. What is the highlight of Nebraskaland Days held in North Platte every June?

A. Four-day Buffalo Bill Rodeo.

———∞———

Q. What Nebraska City observance celebrates the apple harvest in late September?

A. Applejack Festival.

Q. Where is Chevyland U.S.A., a collection of over 110 restored Chevrolets from 1914 to 1974?

A. Elm Creek.

Q. What four-day celebration held in Gering every July features an old settler's reunion, parades, street dances, concerts, and an art show?

A. Oregon Trail Days.

Q. In Gothenburg, what event in early fall celebrates the city's frontier heritage?

A. Harvest Festival.

Q. The Stuhr Museum of the Prairie Pioneer in Grand Island contains the restored cottage in which what famous actor was born?

A. Henry Fonda, in 1914.

HISTORY

Q. Who was the first woman mayor of Lincoln and also the first woman president of the U.S. Conference of Mayors?

A. Helen Boosalis.

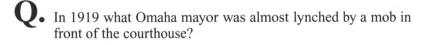

Q. In 1919 what Omaha mayor was almost lynched by a mob in front of the courthouse?

A. Ed Smith.

Q. How many people were killed in Omaha's tornado of 1975?

A. Three.

Q. During World War II German prisoners of war were kept at what camp near Holdrege?

A. Camp Atlanta.

Q. Who sent Lewis and Clark up the Missouri River and across the Rocky Mountains to the Pacific Coast?

A. Thomas Jefferson.

Q. When did President Franklin Pierce sign the Kansas-Nebraska Act creating the vast Nebraska Territory extending north to Canada?

A. 1854.

———∞———

Q. What former Omahan founded a California savings and loan company bearing his name which sold for $10 billion in 1998?

A. H. F. Ahmanson.

———∞———

Q. The *Omaha World-Herald* credited whom for ending the violent 1935 street car strike in Omaha?

A. Gov. Roy Cochran.

———∞———

Q. Attendance at Omaha's 1898 Trans-Mississippi Exposition hit a peak of almost one hundred thousand when what president appeared?

A. William McKinley.

———∞———

Q. In 1949 what milling company sold the rights to use "Gold Medal" to General Mills for five thousand dollars?

A. Neligh Mills.

———∞———

Q. Neligh's Gates College merged in 1915 with what larger Nebraska college?

A. Doane.

———∞———

Q. What Spanish fur trader from Saint Louis built a trading post on the Missouri River north of present-day Omaha?

A. Manuel Lisa.

Q. What was the largest fort in the West, built in 1820 on the site where Lewis and Clark had held a council with the Indians (near today's Omaha)?

A. Fort Atkinson.

Q. In 1806 on his way to the Rockies where a mountain was named for him, what army officer stopped in Nebraska?

A. Lt. Zebulon Pike.

Q. What military explorer in 1823 labeled the plains, including Nebraska, "the great American desert"?

A. Maj. Stephen H. Long.

Q. What artist documented the scientific Maximilian Expedition up the Missouri River in 1833-34?

A. Karl Bodmer.

Q. What brother of a Revolutionary War general played a key role in the early exploration of Nebraska?

A. Capt. William Clark of the Lewis and Clark Expedition (brother of Gen. George Rogers Clark).

Q. Before the railroads, what was the principal method of getting to Nebraska?

A. Steamboat.

Q. Who was the South Carolina politician who died two days after becoming the first territorial governor of Nebraska?

A. Francis Burt.

Q. What governor decreed that the territorial assembly would meet in Omaha rather than Bellevue, thus making Omaha the state's major metropolis?

A. Thomas Cuming.

Q. Where in Omaha was the first territorial capitol built?

A. Ninth and Farnam Streets.

Q. By 1860 what was the population of Omaha?

A. Close to thirty thousand.

Q. The 1860-61 Pony Express route to the West Coast passed through Nebraska after originating in what town?

A. Saint Joseph, Missouri.

Q. When did construction begin on the Union Pacific Railroad westward from Omaha?

A. 1865.

Q. Who was the first person in the nation to acquire land (near Beatrice) under the Homestead Act of 1862?

A. Daniel Freeman.

Q. Who became a major general in the Civil War and later was senator and governor of Nebraska?

A. John M. Thayer.

Q. The sixteen-year-old son of what Omaha meatpacking millionaire was kidnapped in 1890 and held until a $25,000 ransom was paid?

A. Edward Cudahy.

Q. What name was given to the incident near present-day Lexington in which Indians killed at least a dozen members of a wagon train?

A. Plum Creek Massacre.

Q. In 1877 what famous Ogalala Sioux was killed while trying to escape from custody at Fort Robinson?

A. Crazy Horse.

Q. What important governmental building once stood on the site of Omaha Central High School?

A. Nebraska's second territorial capitol.

Q. In 1871 what state governor was removed from office by the legislature for misappropriating funds?

A. David Butler.

Q. Where was the 1892 national convention of the Populist Party held?

A. Omaha.

Q. Three-time presidential candidate William Jennings Bryan worked for a short period as editorial writer for what newspaper?

A. *Omaha World-Herald.*

Q. Who was the political "boss" of Omaha until the early 1930s?

A. Tom Dennison.

Q. Who was known as "the Cowboy Mayor" of Omaha?

A. Jim Dahlman.

Q. When did the Union Pacific complete its railroad bridge across the Missouri River?

A. 1872.

Q. What two residents of Lincoln with the same first name ran against each other as candidates for vice president in 1924?

A. Charles W. Bryan and Charles G. Dawes.

Q. What graduate of Omaha Creighton Prep became the Air Force chief of staff, a position once held by his father?

A. Gen. Michael Ryan.

Q. William H. Thompson, dean of the College of Arts and Sciences at the University of Omaha, was the father-in-law of what prominent Omahan?

A. Warren Buffett.

Q. What South Omaha grocer became mayor of Omaha?

A. Al Veys.

Q. What University of Nebraska graduate served as Franklin D. Roosevelt's first secretary of war?

A. George Dern.

Q. What Omaha businessman served as Harry Truman's secretary of the navy?

A. Francis P. Matthews.

Q. What former resident of Falls City and University of Nebraska graduate became attorney general of the United States?

A. Herbert Brownell.

Q. What former commandant of cadets at the University of Nebraska later became general of the armies, the highest rank thus far bestowed?

A. John J. Pershing.

Q. What Nebraska governor published the *Nebraska Farmer*?

A. Samuel R. McKelvie.

Q. In the 1930s what economic group attempted to raise prices by withholding its products from the market?

A. Farmers.

Q. During 1934-36 what natural disaster blew into Nebraska?

A. Dust storms.

Q. What Nebraska town was famed for its hospitality to troops at its railroad station in World War II?

A. North Platte.

Q. How many air bases were built in Nebraska during World War II?

A. Eleven.

Q. How many Nebraskans lost their lives while in military service during World War II?

A. 3,839.

Q. What officer from North Platte commanded Nebraska's 134th Infantry Regiment in World War II?

A. Butler B. Miltonberger.

Q. Where in Nebraska were ordnance plants built during World War II?

A. Grand Island, Hastings, Sidney, and Mead.

Q. An army base south of Omaha was named for what Civil War general?

A. George Crook.

Q. At what military base did the army establish a dog training center in 1942?

A. Fort Robinson.

Q. Credit is given to what senator for bringing the headquarters of the Strategic Air Command to Omaha in 1948?

A. Kenneth Wherry.

Q. What legendary cigar-smoking World War II hero commanded the Strategic Air Command after it moved to Omaha?

A. Curtis LeMay.

Q. First elected in 1960, what Democratic governor served three two-year terms?

A. Frank Morrison.

Q. What governor said that signing the death warrant for killer Charles Starkweather was the most difficult act of his administration?

A. Ralph Brooks.

Q. What Republican governor spearheaded the campaign to impose state income and sales taxes?

A. Norbert Tiemann.

Q. The beaming countenance of what hardware merchant and Republican governor earned him the nickname "Smiley"?

A. Victor E. Anderson.

Q. Who was the 1944 Democratic candidate for governor whose platform was to square the circle?

A. George Olson.

Q. What governor's wife used to slide down the bannister in the Governor's Mansion?

A. Ruth Thone.

Q. What president-to-be rode the train from Kansas City to Omaha to play poker with his cronies in the Paxton Hotel?

A. Harry Truman.

Q. In 1985 Governor Kerrey escorted what actress while she was in Lincoln for the filming of *Terms of Endearment*?

A. Debra Winger.

Q. Before winning elective office himself, first as a congressman, then as governor, who served as aide to Sen. Roman Hruska?

A. Charles Thone.

Q. The first lawsuit in Nebraska concerned what stolen object?

A. Cheese.

Q. The name *Nebraska* is the English translation of the Oto Indian word *nebrathka* meaning what?

A. "Flat water" (applied to the Platte River).

Q. What was the name of William F. "Buffalo Bill" Cody's seven-thousand-acre cattle ranch near North Platte?

A. Scouts Rest.

Q. What town was the northern terminus of the Chisholm Trail on which cattle were brought up from Texas?

A. Schuyler.

———∞∞∞———

Q. What bank issued its own currency in the 1850s to finance land speculation?

A. Bank of Florence.

———∞∞∞———

Q. Now part of Omaha, what is the name of the place where more than six hundred Mormons died from the cold on their trek west?

A. Winter Quarters.

———∞∞∞———

Q. At Rock Creek in 1861, who shot and killed David McCanles, the owner of a Pony Express relay station?

A. James Butler "Wild Bill" Hickock.

———∞∞∞———

Q. The trial in Omaha of what Ponca Indian chief did much to improve legal rights for all Indians?

A. Standing Bear.

———∞∞∞———

Q. What was the last name of the three brothers from Niobrara—Gary, Gregory, and Kelly—who died when their destroyer went down off Vietnam in 1969?

A. Sage.

———∞∞∞———

Q. What town on the Missouri River was the home of both candidates for governor in 1872?

A. Brownville.

Q. What brothers from Columbus headed the legendary Pawnee Scouts, Indians who helped the army and protected the railroad?

A. Frank and Luther North.

Q. The *Bertrand,* one of more than four hundred steamships wrecked on the Missouri River, was recovered intact in 1969 at what wildlife refuge north of Omaha?

A. DeSoto Bend.

Q. For what Revolutionary War figure was Wayne County named?

A. Gen. "Mad" Anthony Wayne.

Q. What general stopped off in Nebraska to campaign against the Sioux and Cheyenne near Fort McPherson in 1867?

A. George Armstrong Custer.

Q. With its steep cliffs but good water supply, what picturesque canyon was both an obstacle and a blessing to pioneers?

A. Ash Hollow.

Q. What became the Nebraska terminus of the cattle trail from Texas after it was relocated to the west by the settlement of eastern Kansas and Oklahoma?

A. Ogallala.

Q. The victims of the brawling in Ogallala's cowboy heyday were buried in what cemetery?

A. Boot Hill.

Q. What Civil War general selected the site for Fort Hartsuff on the North Loup River to protect settlers?

A. Gen. O. E. C. Ord.

———⚬⚬⚬———

Q. Who was the ringleader of the biggest robbery of a Union Pacific train, which took place in 1877 at Big Springs?

A. Sam Bass.

———⚬⚬⚬———

Q. Where in Omaha did a World War II Japanese balloon bomb explode on April 18, 1945, after crossing the Pacific Ocean and Rocky Mountains?

A. Fiftieth Street and Underwood Avenue.

———⚬⚬⚬———

Q. In the backyard of what Omaha attorney did John F. Kennedy give a campaign speech in 1960?

A. Bernard Boyle.

———⚬⚬⚬———

Q. What name was given to President Gerald Ford upon his birth in Omaha?

A. Leslie King Jr.

———⚬⚬⚬———

Q. What former mayor of Sidney became publisher of the *Omaha World-Herald*?

A. John Gottschalk.

———⚬⚬⚬———

Q. Eamon de Valera, Woodrow Wilson, William Jennings Bryan, and Buffalo Bill Cody attended social gatherings in the home of what South Omaha contractor?

A. George Parks.

Q. Grand Duke Alexis of Russia, Gen. William T. Sherman, and Buffalo Bill hunted buffalo together near what town in 1873?

A. Hayes Center.

Q. After leading a forty-five-man expedition to a point near the present site of Columbus, what Spanish explorer was killed by Pawnees in 1720?

A. Lt. Col. Pedro de Villasur.

Q. Who were the *Omaha World-Herald*'s war correspondents in World War II?

A. Lawrence Youngman and Bill Billotte.

Q. What governor of Nebraska claimed a world's record by speaking 487 words in a minute on a radio station?

A. Ralph Brooks.

Q. What senator collapsed and died shortly after finishing a singing act at the Omaha Press Club Ball?

A. Edward Zorinsky.

Q. Who are the only two Nebraska congressmen who have died in office?

A. George Heinke and Karl Stefan.

Q. What former Democratic congressman from California graduated from Omaha's Benson High School?

A. Walter Capps.

Q. What is Nebraska's oldest town, founded in 1822 by agents of the Missouri Fur Company?

A. Bellevue.

Q. What influential Omaha chief was the son of fur trader Lucien Fontenelle?

A. Logan Fontenelle.

Q. What leading Bellevue resident established a ferry across the Missouri River in the 1840s?

A. Peter Sarpy.

Q. Gen. John C. Frémont, for whom Fremont was named, had what nickname?

A. "The Pathfinder."

Q. Who were the first missionaries in Bellevue?

A. Moses and Eliza Merrill.

Q. What Catholic missionary order built its headquarters on a hill overlooking Bellevue?

A. Columban Fathers.

Q. Based in Nebraska City, what was the largest freight firm in the West?

A. Russell, Majors, and Waddell.

Q. What Illinois senator helped push the Kansas-Nebraska Act of 1854 through Congress and gave his name to the county that contains Omaha?

A. Stephen A. Douglas.

Q. Congress overrode whose presidential veto to make Nebraska a state?

A. Andrew Johnson.

Q. Where did members of the legislature who wanted to move the capital from Omaha to Lancaster County hold a rump session?

A. Florence.

Q. In 1867 a commission considered Ashland, Yankee Hill, Saline City, and Lincoln as possible sites for what building?

A. The state capitol.

Q. What famous Oglala chief won concessions from President Ulysses S. Grant and made a triumphal tour of New York?

A. Red Cloud.

Q. What was the battle that ended the conflict between the U.S. Army and the Indians of the North Plains?

A. Wounded Knee.

Q. Gen. George Crook persuaded what newspaper editor to publicize Standing Bear's fight for Indian rights?

A. Thomas Tibbles.

Q. What Indian woman married Omaha journalist Thomas Tibbles and is now in the Nebraska Hall of Fame?

A. Susette La Flesche (Bright Eyes).

———∞———

Q. In 1992 who was the first Nebraskan to make a serious run for the presidency since George Norris?

A. Robert Kerrey.

———∞———

Q. How many people saw Buffalo Bill's Wild West Show during the Trans-Mississippi Exposition in Omaha on August 31, 1898?

A. Twenty-four thousand.

———∞———

Q. What fueled the first trains of the Union Pacific Railroad?

A. Green cottonwood.

———∞———

Q. The Union Pacific received what percentage of the state's total land from the federal government?

A. Around 10 percent.

———∞———

Q. How long did a homesteader have to live on the land before he could acquire title?

A. Five years.

———∞———

Q. How many homesteaders did Nebraska have by 1900?

A. Close to sixty-nine thousand—the most among all the states.

Q. Who founded the Union Stockyards in South Omaha and later became a congressman?

A. John McShane.

Q. What organization of farmers formed in the 1860s to promote their economic and political goals?

A. The Grange.

Q. What Populist candidate for president won almost 42 percent of the vote in Nebraska in 1892?

A. James B. Weaver.

Q. What farm protest movement blocked shipment of crops from Iowa into Omaha in 1932?

A. Farmers' Holiday Association.

Q. Who was known as "the Boy Orator of the Platte" and "The Great Commoner"?

A. William Jennings Bryan.

Q. What future general taught math to future novelists Willa Cather and Dorothy Canfield Fisher at the University of Nebraska?

A. John J. Pershing.

Q. What future governor of Nebraska served under Gen. John J. Pershing when he headed the expedition that chased Pancho Villa in Mexico?

A. Dwight Griswold.

Q. What senator from Nebraska was among six to vote against declaring war on Germany in 1917?

A. George W. Norris.

Q. How many Nebraskans served in the armed forces during World War I?

A. Almost forty-eight thousand.

Q. What was the first city in the country to fulfill its quota of war bonds in World War I?

A. Omaha.

Q. Before founding Boys Town, who interrupted his studies in Rome to work as a bookkeeper at Cudahy's packing plant in Omaha?

A. Rev. Edward J. Flanagan.

Q. What University of Nebraska political scientist was advisor in the formation of the unicameral legislature?

A. John P. Senning.

Q. How many of the twelve thousand prisoners of war held in Nebraska camps during World War II managed successful escapes?

A. One.

Q. In 1992 what military organization replaced the Strategic Air Command as a tenant at Offutt Air Force Base?

A. U.S. Strategic Command.

Q. In 1895 what was Nebraska's nickname?

A. The Tree Planters' State.

———∞———

Q. For many years what Nebraska college graduated more future generals than any other school except West Point?

A. University of Nebraska at Omaha.

———∞———

Q. At what Omaha store did George Patton, Ronald Reagan, and some of the astronauts buy boots?

A. Dehner Boot Company.

———∞———

Q. What year was the name Cornhusker officially adopted by the state legislature?

A. 1945.

———∞———

Q. What former operator of an office supply business in Lincoln became governor and served three terms in the U.S. Senate?

A. J. J. Exon.

———∞———

Q. What was the birth name of Omaha native Malcolm X?

A. Malcolm Little.

———∞———

Q. What former University of Nebraska president became secretary of agriculture?

A. Clifford Hardin.

Q. What prominent Omaha businessman's murder in Hanscom Park on December 22, 1931, had political repercussions?

A. Harry Lapidus.

———∞———

Q. What Omaha general was U.S. commander in the China theater in 1944, was advisor to Premier Chiang Kai-Shek, and made a brief attempt to run for president?

A. Albert C. Wedemeyer.

———∞———

Q. What Platte Center native was supreme commander of NATO and also refereed international bridge tournaments?

A. Gen. Alfred M. Gruenther.

———∞———

Q. When did Gen. Mark Clark, commander of Allied forces in Italy during World War II, serve a hitch with the Seventh Corps in Omaha?

A. 1935-36.

———∞———

Q. What Boys Town graduate was captain of the USS Pueblo when it was captured by North Koreans in January 1968?

A. Lloyd Bucher.

———∞———

Q. In 1961 what native of Lincoln became mayor of Los Angeles?

A. Sam Yorty.

———∞———

Q. Who was John F. Kennedy's Lincoln-born speech writer and political strategist?

A. Ted Sorensen.

Q. What secretary of commerce under President Nixon was born in Kearney?

A. Peter G. Peterson.

Q. Born in Omaha, what former Florida congressman and prisoner of the North Vietnamese returned to Vietnam as U.S. ambassador?

A. Douglas "Pete" Peterson.

Q. What Omaha native became a Wisconsin congressman and later secretary of defense under President Nixon?

A. Melvin Laird.

Q. What native of Lincoln headed President Ford's White House staff, was secretary of defense, and has been regarded as a possible presidential candidate?

A. Richard Cheney.

Q. What native of Beatrice became ambassador to Ecuador?

A. Charles Brewster.

Q. Where did the first battle between the U.S. Army and the Indians of the North Plains take place?

A. Blue Creek, in 1855.

Q. Born in Plattsmouth, what woman became president of a construction company and served in the U.S. Senate?

A. Hazel Abel.

Q. What younger brother of a presidential candidate served as governor of Nebraska and, in 1924, ran for vice president?

A. Charles W. Bryan.

Q. What congressman from Omaha advocated more attention to the gold standard and was the father of financier Warren Buffett?

A. Howard Buffett.

Q. What Civil War general and builder of the Union Pacific Railroad lived for a time in Omaha and on a farm in Douglas County?

A. Grenville Dodge.

Q. Born in Holdrege, what vice admiral was commanding officer of the USS *Enterprise*?

A. Forrest S. Petersen.

Q. What elected official, born on a Kearney County farm, served forty years in the U.S. Senate and House?

A. Carl Curtis.

Q. Following World War II, what former governor of Nebraska was in charge of the aid program to Greece?

A. Dwight Griswold.

Q. What former Douglas County commissioner served in the U.S. Senate from 1954 to 1976?

A. Roman Hruska.

Q. What president of Latvia graduated from the University of Nebraska and worked for Roberts Dairy while in school?

A. Karl Ulmanis.

Q. The vehicles that brought children from foundling homes in the East to Nebraska and other states for adoption had what nickname?

A. Orphan Trains.

Q. What was the first group that took wagons across the prairie to the Rockies?

A. Sublette Expedition.

Q. Although his monument is in Iowa, where did Charles Floyd, the only man lost by Lewis and Clark, die from appendicitis?

A. The site of South Sioux City.

Q. What Millard South High School teacher was on the team that supervised the municipal elections in Bosnia-Herzegovina in 1997?

A. Sonya Fidler.

Q. What was the original name of the state's capital?

A. Lancaster.

Q. What amateur rodeo rider and son of a Nebraska congressman was President Reagan's secretary of commerce?

A. Malcolm Baldridge.

Q. Who was the first governor of Nebraska to serve a four-year term?

A. Norbert Tiemann.

———

Q. What Nebraska congressman proposed marriage to Miss America, Tara Dawn Holland, at the White House in December 1997?

A. Jon Christensen.

———

Q. Who was the only woman hanged in Nebraska?

A. Elizabeth Taylor, buried near Spring Ranch in Clay County.

———

Q. Who was the first woman governor of Nebraska?

A. Kay Orr (1987–1991).

———

Q. What Hastings publisher was appointed senator in 1951 and later became President Eisenhower's secretary of the interior?

A. Fred Seaton.

———

Q. What chancellor of the University of Nebraska at Omaha served twenty years, the longest of any in the school's ninety-year history?

A. Del Weber.

———

Q. What Omaha attorney and businessman was appointed senator in 1987 by Gov. Kay Orr to succeed Edward Zorinsky?

A. David Karnes.

Q. What Sand Hills rancher became the first woman senator from Nebraska?

A. Eva Bowring.

———⋘———

Q. Who won the Nebraska Republican presidential primary in 1948?

A. Harold Stassen.

———⋘———

Q. In a battle of write-in candidates, who defeated Dwight Eisenhower in the 1952 Nebraska Republican presidential primary?

A. Robert Taft.

———⋘———

Q. What former governor of Nebraska became national civil defense director and ambassador to Denmark and Finland?

A. Val Peterson.

———⋘———

Q. What state senator wears a T-shirt in the legislative chamber?

A. Ernie Chambers.

———⋘———

Q. The governor often bestows what honorary commission upon visiting VIPs?

A. Admiral of the Nebraska Navy.

———⋘———

Q. What contractor bought the *Omaha World-Herald* in 1962 to prevent it from being sold to New York publisher Samuel Newhouse?

A. Peter Kiewit.

Q. What former president of the University of Nebraska became President Bush's administrator of the Agency for International Development?

A. Ronald Roskens.

Q. What former Douglas County sheriff was a Secret Service agent in the White House during the Eisenhower years?

A. Richard Roth.

Q. What native of Eustis became secretary of agriculture and U.S. trade representative?

A. Clayton Yeuter.

Q. What former Nebraskan was director of the Federal Bureau of Investigation?

A. William Sessions.

Q. What 1954 graduate of Omaha's North High School became superintendent of the U.S. Naval Academy?

A. Adm. Charles Larson.

Q. Before being elected to the Senate, what Vietnam veteran Medal of Honor winner served as governor?

A. Robert Kerrey.

Q. In 1987 what senator's wife was appointed to the National Commission on Drug-Free Schools?

A. Liz Karnes.

Q. Before he became mayor of Omaha, what elective political office did Hal Daub hold?

A. U.S. Representative.

———∞∞———

Q. When was a trolley line built from Bellevue to connect with the South Omaha trolleys?

A. 1906.

———∞∞———

Q. Who was the lieutenant governor to succeed Ralph Brooks, the first Nebraska governor to die in office?

A. Dwight Burney.

———∞∞———

Q. What *first* did Ruth Bryan Owen, the daughter of William Jennings Bryan, achieve?

A. First woman minister to a foreign country (Denmark).

———∞∞———

Q. How many men did Nebraska send to fight in the Spanish-American War?

A. Thirty-four hundred.

———∞∞———

Q. What Vietnam veteran struck it rich in the cellular phone business before being elected senator in 1996?

A. Chuck Hagel.

———∞∞———

Q. Born in York, what ten-term congressman has held several committee posts dealing with foreign affairs?

A. Douglas K. Bereuter.

Q. Before going to Washington in 1990, what congressman was speaker of the state legislature?

A. William E. Barrett.

———∞∞∞———

Q. What former Eagle Scout from McCook became state insurance director and later governor of Nebraska?

A. Benjamin Nelson.

———∞∞∞———

Q. In 1795 Spanish interests in Saint Louis sent what Scotsman to head their third expedition up the Missouri River?

A. James Mackay.

———∞∞∞———

Q. What electric supply store owner headed the Omaha City Charter Convention in the 1950s and later became mayor?

A. A. V. Sorensen.

———∞∞∞———

Q. When Gov. Frank Morrison was out of the state in 1966, what lieutenant governor ordered two companies of national guardsmen to Omaha to calm racial disorders?

A. Phil Sorensen.

———∞∞∞———

Q. What woman from Superior, the highest paid female executive in the 1920s, married a British lord to become Lady Vestey?

A. Evelene Brodstone.

———∞∞∞———

Q. What resident of Beemer became national commander of the American Legion in the 1960s?

A. William Galbraith.

Q. What former Lincoln correspondent for the *Omaha World-Herald* and candidate for the Senate became assistant secretary of labor for veterans affairs?

A. Don Shasteen.

Q. A native of Polk and daughter of Congressman John Norton, who was John F. Kennedy's private secretary?

A. Evelyn Lincoln.

Q. Born in Rising City and a former medical missionary in China, what Minnesota congressman was voted one of the five most influential members of the House?

A. Walter Judd.

Q. What member of a prominent Omaha retailing family went down with the *Titanic* in 1912?

A. Emil Brandeis.

Q. What Nebraska delegate nominated a fictional Joe Smith for president at the 1956 Republican National Convention?

A. Terry Carpenter.

Q. What Omaha grain dealer served as senator from 1941 to 1954?

A. Hugh Butler.

Q. President of Peter Kiewit Sons' Inc., contractors, what Omahan has joined *Forbes* magazine's list of billionaires?

A. Walter Scott Jr.

Q. The annual stockholders meeting in Omaha of what company draws investors from all over the world to hear financier Warren Buffett answer questions about the market?

A. Berkshire-Hathaway.

Q. With corporate headquarters in Omaha, what is America's second largest food company?

A. ConAgra.

Q. According to Barron's magazine in 1996, how many employees and retirees of Peter Kiewit Sons' Inc. owned stock positions worth more than $1 million each?

A. About 350.

Q. What Omaha-trained nurse is the sole woman rear admiral in the U.S. Naval Reserve?

A. Karen A. Harmeyer.

Q. What butter, egg, and poultry business founded in Gage County in 1894 later moved to Lincoln and then to Chicago in 1913 to become one of the world's biggest food companies?

A. Beatrice Foods.

Q. What candidate for president of Czechoslovakia in 1992 was managing a restaurant in Wilber in 1998?

A. Victor Z. Prochazka.

Q. In 1997, what Omaha-based business was the world's largest telephone marketing and service company with sixteen thousand employees in thirteen countries?

A. Sitel Inc.

Q. Where does Nebraska rank among states in the production of ethanol, a motor fuel additive made from corn and other grains?

A. Third.

———— ✺ ————

Q. What Omaha Mayor resigned in 1994 to become president of Duncan Aviation in Lincoln?

A. P. J. Morgan.

———— ✺ ————

Q. In 1879 whose trial in Hastings for killing two homesteaders caused Gen. George Crook to send troops from Omaha to quell possible disorders?

A. Print Olive, cattleman.

———— ✺ ————

Q. What outlaw used the Sand Hills as his stamping ground after the Civil War?

A. D. C. "Doc" Middleton.

———— ✺ ————

Q. Where was Nebraska's only volcano, whose fire and smoke were recorded in the journals of Lewis and Clark and has since disappeared?

A. Near Newcastle.

———— ✺ ————

Q. What famous Indian chief is buried near Macy on a hill named for him overlooking the Missouri River?

A. Blackbird.

———— ✺ ————

Q. What city was once the nation's number one meat packing center before the plants were dispersed to rural areas?

A. Omaha.

Q. What former teacher in the Lincoln Public Schools is lieutenant governor of Nebraska?

A. Kim Robak.

———∞———

Q. The second floor of the courthouse in what town was blown off by a tornado in 1953 and never restored?

A. Hebron.

———∞———

Q. For what governor is the Highway 20 bridge over the Niobrara River near Valentine named?

A. Charles W. Bryan.

———∞———

Q. What congressman from Fairbury (1967-71) was appointed a federal judge?

A. Robert V. Denney.

———∞———

Q. Who was the first Indian agent at Fort Atkinson, a man whose name was given to a bluff on the Oregon Trail near Sutherland?

A. Benjamin O'Fallon.

———∞———

Q. The Burlington Railroad changed the route of its track in 1899 so it would not cross the grave of what woman who died of cholera on the Mormon Trail in 1852 near present-day Gering?

A. Rebecca Winters.

———∞———

Q. What were the two southeastern Nebraska towns that merged in 1881 to form Auburn?

A. Sheridan and Calvert.

Q. What president made a speech in 1904 from a specially built grandstand near the railroad tracks at Hyannis?

A. Theodore Roosevelt.

Q. When did the *Omaha Bee-News* cease publication, leaving the *Omaha World-Herald* the only daily newspaper in town?

A. 1937.

Q. Premier Indira Gandhi of India was the house guest of what Omaha University faculty member and his wife in 1962?

A. Roderic Crane.

Q. After visiting Nebraska at least twenty times, what outlaw made plans to settle down on a farm near Franklin just before he was shot?

A. Jesse James.

Q. Where did Henry Stanley work as a newspaper correspondent before meeting Dr. David Livingston in Africa?

A. Omaha.

Q. Who ran a notorious house of ill repute across the street from Omaha's Trans-Mississippi Exposition in 1898?

A. The Everleigh sisters, Ada and Minne.

Q. What former Democratic presidential candidate from Illinois graduated from Dana College in Blair?

A. Paul Simon.

ARTS & LITERATURE

C H A P T E R   F O U R

Q. For which novel did Willa Cather win a Pulitzer Prize in 1923?

A. *One of Ours.*

———————

Q. What was the state's first newspaper?

A. The *Nebraska Palladium.*

———————

Q. When did Nebraska poet laureate John G. Neihardt publish his epic poem *The Song of Hugh Glass*?

A. 1915.

———————

Q. What mythical pioneer figure was popularized in the writings of Wayne Carroll and Don Holmes of Gothenburg?

A. Febold Feboldson.

———————

Q. The childhood home of Willa Cather, what town served as the setting for her six Nebraska novels?

A. Red Cloud.

Q. What renowned British architect designed Joslyn Art Museum's $16 million new wing that opened in 1994?

A. Sir Norman Foster.

Q. What renowned artist made drawings and paintings of Nebraska Indians during 1831-32?

A. George Catlin.

Q. What Omaha singer made it to the operatic big leagues— performing at the Met, at La Scala, and across Europe?

A. Alexandra Hunt.

Q. What Omaha painter gained a reputation for his portraits of William Jennings Bryan?

A. J. Laurie Wallace.

Q. Sculptor Daniel Chester French created the statue of what president on the west side of the state capitol?

A. Abraham Lincoln.

Q. What Nebraska lawyer/botanist became dean of the Harvard Law School?

A. Roscoe Pound.

Q. Born in Sheridan County, who wrote the book *Old Jules,* a story about her crusty pioneer father?

A. Mari Sandoz.

Q. Who wrote *Oregon Trail,* which dealt with the eastern end of the pathway—Nebraska, Kansas, and Missouri?

A. Francis Parkman.

Q. Who was the first Catholic missionary in Nebraska and author of a book about the wilderness, *Letters and Sketches*?

A. Father Peter de Smet.

Q. While raising four children as a widow in Elmwood, what author wrote best-selling novels and short stories?

A. Bess Streeter Aldrich.

Q. Who was the editor and one of the founders of the magazine *American Speech*?

A. Louise Pound.

Q. What college in Fremont was founded in Atchison, Kansas?

A. Midland Lutheran College.

Q. In 1882 who became the first president of Hastings College?

A. Dr. W. F. Ringland.

Q. Which of Nebraska's ranking artists moved to Guatemala and switched from painting midwestern barns to depicting tropical volcanoes?

A. Dale Nichols.

Q. What son of author Bess Streeter Aldrich became a writer of western stories and a newspaper columnist in Los Gatos, California?

A. Robert Aldrich.

Q. Who founded the Western Newspaper Union and was memorialized by Omaha's art museum?

A. George A. Joslyn.

Q. What *Omaha World-Herald* photographer won a Pulitzer Prize for his picture of an officer returning to his family from World War II?

A. Earle "Buddy" Bunker.

Q. What former publisher of the *Omaha World-Herald* was chairman of the World Press Freedom Committee?

A. Harold W. Andersen.

Q. Paderewski, Caruso, and Sarah Bernhardt appeared on-stage at what former Omaha building at Fourteenth and Howard Streets?

A. Municipal Auditorium.

Q. How much was Oscar Wilde paid for making a speech in Omaha in 1882?

A. $250.

Q. In what year did the *Evening World* and the *Daily Herald* merge to become the *Omaha World-Herald*?

A. 1889.

Q. What wife of a Wyoming ranch manager has written a 392-page paperback, *Roadside History of Nebraska*?

A. Candy Moulton.

———

Q. What institution occupies the former Union Passenger Terminal of the Union Pacific Railroad in Omaha?

A. Durham Western Heritage Museum.

———

Q. What group of singers appeared at Omaha's Duchesne Academy in the early 1950s before they were made famous by *The Sound of Music*?

A. Trapp Family Singers.

———

Q. What style of architecture is Omaha's Saint Cecilia's Cathedral?

A. Spanish Renaissance.

———

Q. Who designed the complex of buildings and grounds in Omaha once known as Ak-Sar-Ben Field?

A. Georg B. Prinz.

———

Q. What landscape architectural firm designed the Gerald Ford Birthsite and Gardens in Omaha?

A. Schlott, Farrington, and Associates.

———

Q. What artist from Shelby was known for the covers he painted for the *Omaha World-Herald* supplement, *Magazine of the Midlands*?

A. Terence Duren.

Q. What former art director of the *Omaha World-Herald* has placed 450 of his urban landscapes in collections nationwide?

A. Allan Tubach.

Q. What Cozad native was a founder of the Ash Can School of painting?

A. Robert Henri.

Q. What graduate of Omaha's South High School became a Pulitzer Prize-winning historian at the University of Wisconsin?

A. Merle E. Curti.

Q. What World War I commander won the Pulitzer Prize for history in 1932?

A. Gen. John J. Pershing.

Q. The 1945 Pulitzer Prize for poetry went to what resident of Lincoln?

A. Karl Shapiro.

Q. What was the hometown of poet laureate John G. Neihardt?

A. Bancroft.

Q. The inscriptions on the state capitol were written by what anthropologist, educator, and member of the Nebraska Hall of Fame?

A. Hartley Burr Alexander.

Q. What sculptor, who grew up in Fremont and Omaha, designed the Mount Rushmore National Monument in South Dakota?

A. Gutzon Borglum.

───── ∞ ─────

Q. What founder of the *Omaha World-Herald* later became a senator and powerful figure in Washington?

A. Gilbert M. Hitchcock.

───── ∞ ─────

Q. At the John G. Neihardt Center in Bancroft what symbolizes the poet laureate's interest in American Indian customs and traditions?

A. Sacred Hoop Garden.

───── ∞ ─────

Q. Born in West Point, what University of Chicago historian has written more than forty-five books?

A. Martin Marty.

───── ∞ ─────

Q. Who is the first woman president of Nebraska Wesleyan University in Lincoln?

A. Dr. Jeanie Watson.

───── ∞ ─────

Q. Who is composer-in-residence at the University of Nebraska?

A. Randall Snyder.

───── ∞ ─────

Q. In 1997 Swiss filmmaker Karl Saurer made a documentary about Swiss immigrants in what Nebraska town?

A. Steinauer.

Q. Who wrote the book *The Necessity of Empty Places* about a trek from Minnesota through Nebraska to Montana?

A. Paul Gruchow.

Q. Who was the first curator of Omaha's Bemis Center for Contemporary Art?

A. Steve Joy.

Q. How many opera houses were in Nebraska in its early days, according to Opera Omaha?

A. Around five hundred.

Q. Opera Omaha observes what anniversary in 1998?

A. Fortieth.

Q. In 1997 who chaired the committee that recommended Omaha build a $275 million entertainment arena?

A. David Sokol.

Q. What novelist was the daughter of a president of the University of Nebraska?

A. Dorothy Canfield Fisher.

Q. The book *The Immense Journey* sold more than a million copies and brought national prominence to what Nebraska author?

A. Loren Eiseley.

Q. Who was Omaha's first physician, a man who later turned to journalism and founded the *Omaha Daily Herald* in 1865?

A. George L. Miller.

Q. What U.S. ambassador to Great Britain and former Lincoln resident composed "Melody in A Major," also known as "It's All in the Game"?

A. Charles G. Dawes.

Q. Who were the chief painters of the original murals in the state capitol?

A. Augustus V. Tack and Elizabeth H. Dolan.

Q. What architect of the state capitol died at the age of fifty-four before the building was completed?

A. Bertram Goodhue.

Q. In 1897 what University of Nebraska scholar became a ranking U.S. woman tennis player?

A. Louise Pound.

Q. In hopes of becoming a doctor, what Nebraska author took science courses at the University of Nebraska?

A. Willa Cather.

Q. What Sand Hills author was not allowed by her father to attend school until she was nine years old?

A. Mari Sandoz.

Q. What two Mari Sandoz novels were banned in Omaha and stirred opposition in Lincoln because of their language and violence?

A. *Slogum House* and *Capital City.*

Q. To help pay for his education, what writer rang the class bell at Nebraska Normal College, now Wayne State College?

A. John Neihardt.

Q. What Creighton University professor is co-general editor of the collected works of Henry James?

A. Greg Zacharias.

Q. What performing artists of Mannheim Steamroller also direct Soli Deo Gloria Cantorum, Nebraska's only fully professional chorale?

A. Jackson and Almeda Berkey.

Q. What is the nickname of the Rose Blumkin Performing Arts Center, which houses the Omaha Theater Company for Young People?

A. The Rose.

Q. Both in physical size and number of subscriptions, what is the largest community theater in the nation?

A. Omaha Community Playhouse.

Q. According to *Billboard* magazine, what Omaha-based musical group is the number one Christmas performer in America?

A. Mannheim Steamroller.

Q. Where in Omaha's Old Market do artists from around the world take up residence to perfect their skills?

A. Bemis Center for Contemporary Arts.

———

Q. What is the largest Black-American historical and cultural institution west of the Mississippi River?

A. Great Plains Black History Museum, in Omaha.

———

Q. Lincoln resident Cliff Hillegass wrote what popular series of educational aids?

A. *Cliff's Notes.*

———

Q. What group stages theatrical productions in a former church in Brownville?

A. Village Theater.

———

Q. Where does the Post Playhouse Summer Repertory Theater offer stage productions?

A. Fort Robinson.

———

Q. What Omaha artist created six bronze statues for the World War II Fiftieth Anniversary Memorial in the Heartland of America Park?

A. John Lajba.

———

Q. What world-famous puppeteer came from Grand Island?

A. Bil Baird.

Q. What former vice chancellor of the University of Nebraska at Omaha wrote the 155-page book *Lower Moments in Higher Education*?

A. Otto Bauer.

Q. What University of Nebraska biology professor wrote the well-regarded *Keith County Journal*?

A. John Janovy Jr.

Q. What resident conductor of the Omaha Symphony takes thirty-eight musicians on the road each year to Nebraska communities?

A. Ernest Richardson.

Q. What Nebraskan is recognized as a modern dance pioneer?

A. Charles Weidman.

Q. Larry Sommer directed what state historical society before taking charge of Nebraska's society in 1992?

A. Montana's.

Q. The five-cent Nebraska statehood centennial postage stamp issued in 1967 was designed by what Omaha artist?

A. Julian K. Billings.

Q. What Omaha educator and advertising man wrote *Red Hugh, Prince of Donegal*, which was made into a Walt Disney film?

A. Robert T. Reilly.

Q. The city of Omaha received one of the nation's finest private coin collections as a gift from what pioneer Omaha businessman?

A. Byron Reed.

———— ———

Q. What Omaha theater built in 1926 was first called the Riviera, next the Paramount, and then the Astro?

A. Rose Blumkin Performing Arts Center.

———— ———

Q. Once a vaudeville house, what Omaha theater is now home to symphony, opera, and ballet?

A. Orpheum.

———— ———

Q. What two of the opera world's top sopranos performed with Opera Omaha early in their careers?

A. Renee Fleming and Lauren Flanigan.

———— ———

Q. Who is the artistic director and principal conductor of Opera Omaha?

A. Hal France.

———— ———

Q. Hallmark Cards was founded by what three brothers from Norfolk?

A. Rollie, Will, and Joyce Hall.

———— ———

Q. What was the first novel by Omaha author Richard Dooling?

A. *Critical Care.*

Q. As a soloist, Omaha Symphony conductor Victor Yampolsky plays what instrument?

A. Violin.

———∞———

Q. What Omahan is the author of *The Family Compatibility Test*?

A. Susan Adams.

———∞———

Q. What is the name of the executive editor of the *New York Times* who spent part of his childhood in Omaha?

A. Joseph Lelyveld.

———∞———

Q. What Omaha woman wrote several children's books and articles for the *Saturday Evening Post, Woman's Home Companion,* and *Ladies' Home Journal*?

A. Val Teal.

———∞———

Q. Who wrote the poem *Zero Street,* which was inspired by Lincoln's main thoroughfare, 0 Street?

A. Allen Ginsburg.

———∞———

Q. Considered one of America's foremost composers and conductors, what native of Wahoo directed the Eastman School of Music for forty years?

A. Howard H. Hanson.

———∞———

Q. What Nebraska author never allowed her books to be filmed during her lifetime and had all of her letters destroyed?

A. Willa Cather, (1873–1947).

Q. What writer from Humphrey became city editor of the *Omaha World-Herald,* assistant managing editor of *Time,* and a member of President Nixon's staff?

A. James Keogh.

Q. What Omaha trial lawyer and Vietnam veteran has written at least thirty articles on his experiences in the war, some of them published in the *Omaha World-Herald*?

A. James Martin Davis.

Q. What professor of political science at the University of Nebraska at Omaha spent twelve years writing a biography of Omaha political boss Tom Dennison?

A. Orville Menard.

Q. What former *Omaha World-Herald* editorial writer won a Pulitzer Prize with the Saint Louis *Post Dispatch*?

A. Robert Lasch.

Q. Lincoln was the birthplace of what mystery novelist?

A. Mignon Good Eberhart.

Q. A native of Fremont, who was the first president of the Writer's Guild?

A. Keene Abbott.

Q. What *Omaha World-Herald* writer helped found and became manager of Ballet Omaha?

A. Mary Treynor Smith.

Q. Born in Danbury, what Washington columnist was the first woman assigned to cover the House of Representatives?

A. Bess Furman Armstrong.

Q. What graduate of Omaha's Westside High published her first mystery novel titled *Unsolicited*?

A. Julie Wallin Kaewert.

Q. Stained-glass windows at Tiffany's were the work of what muralist from Lincoln?

A. Elizabeth Dolan.

Q. Who was born in Barbados, was a draftsman for the Union Pacific, and became publisher of the *Omaha World-Herald*?

A. Henry Doorly.

Q. What Omaha novelist wrote *Jefferson Selleck* and a column for the *Omaha World-Herald* called "The View from Pigeon Bend"?

A. Carl Jonas.

Q. What Lincoln writer and educator became editor-in-chief of the University of Nebraska Press?

A. Virginia Faulkner.

Q. What writer once headed the University of Missouri and is a former director of the Nebraska State Historical Society?

A. James C. Olson.

Q. What Lincoln author wrote *Island in the Sky* and *Soldier of Fortune*?

A. Ernest Kellogg Gann.

—⊗⊗⊗—

Q. What former *Omaha World-Herald* reporter headed *Time's* Washington Bureau and wrote several books on national politics?

A. Hugh Sidey.

—⊗⊗⊗—

Q. What native of Osceola has paintings on display in Europe and Latin America?

A. Robert Hansen.

—⊗⊗⊗—

Q. What long-time book reviewer for the *Omaha World-Herald* wrote the column "Leaves from a Bookman's Notebook"?

A. Victor P. Hass.

—⊗⊗⊗—

Q. An early influence on Willa Cather, what *Omaha World-Herald* reporter was the first woman journalist in Omaha?

A. Elia Wilkinson Peattie.

—⊗⊗⊗—

Q. Painter Myron Robert Heise of Bancroft did a portrait of what renowned citizen of that same town?

A. John Neihardt.

—⊗⊗⊗—

Q. Patricia McGerr, author of *Catch Me If You Can* and *Seven Deadly Sisters,* was born in what town?

A. Falls City.

Q. What award did the *Omaha Sun* receive in 1972 for an exposé of Boys Town finances, led by the managing editor, Paul N. Williams?

A. Pulitzer Prize.

Q. What was Omaha-born concert pianist Roger Williams' birth name?

A. Louis Jacob Weertz.

Q. What graduate of Omaha Benson High School and University of Nebraska at Omaha painted murals on the four-teenth floor of the state capitol?

A. Steven Roberts.

Q. What is the literary magazine of the University of Nebraska?

A. *Prairie Schooner.*

Q. Who painted *Watching the Cargo by Night* that was donated in 1997 by the Foxley Cattle Company to the Joslyn Art Museum?

A. George Caleb Bingham.

Q. What sculpture is the centerpiece of Lincoln's Madden Garden at Twelfth and Q?

A. *Torn Notebook.*

Q. The popular Kewpie Doll of the early 1900s was the creation of what Omaha sculptor, painter, and author?

A. Rose O'Neill.

Q. Built in 1923, what was the nation's first junior high school?

A. Whittier, in Lincoln.

———— ∞∞ ————

Q. The sixty-piece Heartland of America band, which puts on an annual Christmas show in Omaha, belongs to what branch of the armed forces?

A. Air Force.

———— ∞∞ ————

Q. In what town was Wright Morris, author of *The Field of Vision* and other novels, born?

A. Central City.

———— ∞∞ ————

Q. The museum of Robert Henri is in what town that was founded by his father?

A. Cozad.

———— ∞∞ ————

Q. What contestant from Deshler, sponsored by the *Omaha World-Herald,* won the 1967 National Spelling Bee by spelling *chihuahua* correctly?

A. Jennifer Reinke.

———— ∞∞ ————

Q. What metal statue is on Abbott Drive between downtown Omaha and Eppley Airfield?

A. *Flight of the Crane.*

———— ∞∞ ————

Q. What painter famed for interpreting western landscapes produced some well-known water-colors of the Oregon Trail?

A. Albert Bierstadt.

Q. What Nebraska-born scholar and writer received more than thirty-six honorary degrees?

A. Loren Eiseley.

Q. What 1976 graduate of Omaha Burke High School became a concert pianist?

A. Karen Kushner.

Q. What Grand Island painter has works in the Metropolitan Museum and Library of Congress?

A. Grant Reynard.

Q. The statue atop the state capitol known as the Sower was created by what sculptor?

A. Lee Lawrie.

Q. Alvin Johnson, editor of the *New Republic,* attended what college?

A. University of Nebraska.

Q. What architect designed Grand Island's Stuhr Museum?

A. Edward Durrell Stone.

Q. What frontier photographer took many pictures of families standing in front of sod houses?

A. Solomon Butcher.

Q. Who was the first professor of English literature at the University of Nebraska and the author of *Nebraska Legends and Other Poems*?

A. Orasmus C. Dake.

Q. What Lincoln advertising man wrote the words to the University of Nebraska fight song, "There Is No Place Like Nebraska"?

A. Joyce Ayres.

Q. In what year did the University of Nebraska win the Sudler Trophy for best marching band in America?

A. 1995–96.

Q. A $40 million gift to the University of Nebraska Foundation for the education of speech and hearing impaired came from what source?

A. W. E. Barkley Trust.

Q. Who is the president of the University of Nebraska at Lincoln?

A. Dennis Smith.

Q. Who wrote the University of Nebraska's alma mater with the help of Chancellor James Moeser, a former professor of music?

A. Chip Davis.

Q. Who is the first woman chancellor of the University of Nebraska at Omaha?

A. Nancy Belck.

Q. Who designed the building at Eighteenth and Harney Streets that housed Omaha's main public library from 1893 to 1977?

A. Thomas Kimball.

Q. What enterprise in South Omaha focuses on Hispanic art, culture, and history?

A. El Museo Latino.

Q. The Great Plains Black Museum is on the former site of what communications establishment?

A. Webster Telephone Exchange.

Q. What *Omaha World-Herald* sports editor and columnist received the Jewish Federation of Omaha's Humanitarian Award for his articles on the plight of the Jewish people in the Soviet Union?

A. Wally Provost.

Q. Joslyn Castle, former home of businessman George Joslyn and now a museum, was once headquarters for what educational body?

A. Omaha Public Schools.

Q. What editorial cartoonist, who was raised in Hastings, won Pulitzer Prizes in 1922, 1925, and 1929 for the New York *World*?

A. Rollin Kirby.

Q. For one hundred years what has been the top social event in Omaha?

A. Ak-Sar-Ben Coronation Ball.

Q. For several years who was the musical arranger and librarian for the Omaha Symphony?

A. Matthew Naughtin.

———∞∞———

Q. What *Omaha World-Herald* photographer wound up his career with eight years as a state senator?

A. John Savage.

———∞∞———

Q. What past president of the Omaha Bar Association wrote a book of witticisms called *The Best of the Cockle Bur*?

A. Harry Otis.

———∞∞———

Q. Who was probably the best-known figure in the Omaha arts community during the eleven years (1984–95) that he was artistic director of the Omaha Symphony?

A. Bruce Hangen.

———∞∞———

Q. What Omaha architect designed the Joslyn Castle, Joslyn Art Museum, and Benson High School?

A. John J. McDonald.

———∞∞———

Q. What artist and former executive director of the Nebraska Arts Council that also served as one of the art critics for the *Omaha World-Herald* for thirty years starting in the late 1930s?

A. Leonard Thiessen.

———∞∞———

Q. What former conductor of the Omaha Symphony lived in Perugia, Italy, after leaving Omaha?

A. Thomas Briccetti.

Q. What roles did Robert Vickrey and Thomas Enckell play on the Omaha cultural scene in the 1970s and 1980s?

A. Ballet artistic directors.

Q. What Vienna-born concert pianist and his pianist wife were popular performers at Omaha's Blackstone Hotel and the Silver Lining Lounge?

A. Robert and Bertie Hellmann.

Q. What Nebraska author of 11 novels and 160 short stories sold every one she ever wrote?

A. Bess Streeter Aldrich.

Q. What native Omahan who went to Westside High co-founded *Spy* magazine and became editor-in-chief of *New York* magazine?

A. Kurt Andersen.

Q. What editor of the *Omaha World-Herald* Magazine of the Midland wrote books about Omaha hospitals, Peter Kiewit Sons' Inc., and Nebraska football?

A. Hollis Limprecht.

Q. Books for young people, such as *Swamp Fox* and *Young Nathan,* are two of some twenty books by what Peru State College graduate?

A. Marion Marsh Brown.

Q. What is the state's oldest newspaper in continuous publication?

A. The *Nebraska City News-Press.*

Q. In 1943 the *Omaha World-Herald* won the Pulitzer Prize for meritorious public service for what endeavor?

A. Leadership in a scrap drive for World War II.

Q. What graduate of Omaha North High School paints angels in New York on collectors' plates for the Bradford Exchange?

A. Edgar Jerins.

Q. Who has been concert master of the Omaha Symphony for the past several years?

A. Richard Lohmann.

Q. What 1979 graduate of Creighton University wrote his first novel, *Desperadoes,* about the Dalton gang?

A. Ron Hansen.

Q. What Omaha painter created abstract murals for the lobbies of some of Omaha's biggest businesses?

A. Bill Farmer.

Q. Compared with other U.S. cathedrals, how does Omaha's Saint Cecilia's Cathedral rank in size?

A. Top ten.

Q. What Civil War general's home in Omaha is now a museum of the Douglas County Historical Society?

A. George Crook.

Q. How many stamps from the Trans-Mississippi Exposition have been reissued to commemorate its one hundredth anniversary in 1998?

A. Nine.

———⁂———

Q. What is Nebraska's motto?

A. Equality before the law.

———⁂———

Q. Born and raised in Lincoln, what University of Pennsylvania author and anthropologist is in Nebraska's Hall of Fame?

A. Loren Eiseley.

———⁂———

Q. Books on the humor in everyday living, such as *Life Is What Happens When You Are Making Other Plans,* gained fame for what Omaha writer?

A. Teresa Bloomingdale.

———⁂———

Q. Who was the first Nebraska composer to win the Omaha Symphony Guild's International New Music Competition with his work *Threnos* for cello and orchestra?

A. Tyler White.

———⁂———

Q. What Creighton University Jesuit priest and sculptor created the bust of Gerald Ford that is displayed at his birthsite?

A. Rev. Jonathan Haschka.

———⁂———

Q. What former social secretary for Jackie Kennedy and daughter of a Nebraska congressman writes a syndicated manners column?

A. Letitia Baldridge.

Q. What is the second largest newspaper in Nebraska?

A. *Lincoln Journal Star.*

Q. What Italian-born painter, who also lived in Venezuela and Acapulco, was one of Omaha's premier art teachers?

A. Oscar Sormani.

Q. What former bullwhacker on the Oregon Trail became a photographer in Omaha whose clients included the Union Pacific and National Geological Survey?

A. William Henry Jackson.

Q. Born in Osceola, what impressionist painter and art teacher "flirted with national acclaim," according to the *Omaha World-Herald*?

A. Augustus Dunbier.

Q. What *Omaha World-Herald* editor won a Pulitzer Prize for his editorial "The Law of the Jungle" about the 1919 lynching in front of the courthouse?

A. Harvey Newbranch.

Q. What well-known poet was on the staff of the *Lincoln Journal*?

A. Walt Mason.

Q. Charles S. Rychman, editorial writer for what newspaper, won a Pulitzer Prize in 1931 for his analysis of the continued reelections of Sen. George Norris?

A. *Fremont Tribune.*

Q. After he retired, what University of Nebraska president (1969–1977) was instrumental in creating the Mid-America Arts Alliance of Kansas City and the Lied Performing Arts Center in Lincoln?

A. Durward "Woody" Varner.

———

Q. Why did historian Bernard DeVoto once have himself dunked in the Missouri River at Plattsmouth?

A. To re-enact a spring ritual of pioneer days.

———

Q. What Nebraska historian was the author of *The Great Platte River Road*?

A. Merrill J. Mattes.

———

Q. What publisher of the *McCook Daily Gazette* said: "Service is the daily price we pay for the space we occupy in this world"?

A. Harry Strunk.

———

Q. What town commemorates the famous novelist Willa Cather with a 610-acre tract of native grassland—Willa Cather Memorial Prairie?

A. Red Cloud.

———

Q. What past president of the Omaha Community Playhouse is a member of the Nebraska Supreme Court?

A. D. Nick Caporale.

———

Q. What late nineteenth century illustrator, lecturer, and writer was known as "Bright Eyes"?

A. Susette LaFlesche Tibbles.

SPORTS & LEISURE

C H A P T E R F I V E

Q. Who coached the Omaha Racers professional basketball team for eight seasons?

A. Mike Thibault.

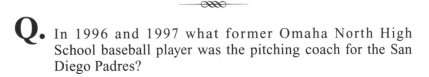

Q. What University of Nebraska sprinter wore sun glasses in his races and won a gold medal in the Mexico City Olympics?

A. Charlie Greene.

Q. How many players are in the Greater Omaha Dart League?

A. Seven hundred.

Q. In 1996 and 1997 what former Omaha North High School baseball player was the pitching coach for the San Diego Padres?

A. Dan Warthen.

Q. What 1955 and 1958 National League batting champion from Tilden died of a heart attack in 1997?

A. Richie Ashburn.

Q. All Nebraskans, Sam Crawford, Bob Gibson, Grover Cleveland Alexander, and Richie Ashburn are in the hall of fame for what sport?

A. Baseball.

Q. What woman basketball player who is third on the Creighton University all-time scoring list with 2,010 points now coaches the team?

A. Connie Yori.

Q. The University of Nebraska at Omaha started playing what Division I sport on October 17, 1997?

A. Ice hockey.

Q. How many years did Tom Osborne serve as head football coach of the University of Nebraska before his retirement in 1998?

A. Twenty-five.

Q. In what years did Tom Osborne's Nebraska football teams win national titles?

A. 1994, 1995, and 1997.

Q. Who was the first student athlete coached by Tom Osborne to graduate with a 4.0 grade point average?

A. Rob Zatechka.

Q. Who was Nebraska football coach Tom Osborne's roommate when they played with the San Francisco 49ers?

A. Jack Kemp.

Q. Where did Bob Devaney coach immediately before coming to the University of Nebraska?

A. University of Wyoming.

Q. Who coaches both the men's and the women's swimming teams at the University of Nebraska?

A. Cal Bentz.

Q. The varsity and junior varsity teams of Nebraska men's gymnastic coach Francis Allen have won how many national titles?

A. Eight.

Q. What 1934 heavyweight boxing champion was born in South Omaha?

A. Max Baer.

Q. What former Nebraska football kicker plays major-league baseball with Anaheim?

A. Darin Erstad.

Q. What former Nebraska basketball star was an outfielder for the New York Yankees?

A. Bob Cerv.

Q. Where was the home of Shade On, the stallion that was the leading money-winning pacer of the nation in 1899?

A. Neligh.

Q. What former caddie at Omaha's Field Club won the U.S. Open in 1933 and the National Amateur in 1937?

A. Johnny Goodman.

Q. What running back from Omaha's Benson High School won the Heisman Trophy with the University of Iowa in 1939 and died in World War II?

A. Nile Kinnick.

Q. What were the most touchdowns scored in a single game by Omaha Central graduate Gale Sayers for the Chicago Bears?

A. Six.

Q. While with the Saint Louis Cardinals, what pitcher from Omaha's Tech High School won the Cy Young Award twice?

A. Bob Gibson (in 1968 and 1970).

Q. Bob Boozer, the Omaha Tech basketball player who starred in the NBA and the Olympics, played for what college?

A. Kansas State.

Q. What former Creighton University baseball player catches for the Chicago Cubs?

A. Scott Servais.

Q. With what major-league team did Omaha Benson High School graduate Jackie Brandt win a Golden Glove award in 1959?

A. San Francisco Giants.

Q. What was the hometown of Saint Louis Cardinals star hitter Johnny Hopp?

A. Hastings.

―――∞∞∞―――

Q. What Omaha-native threw a no-hitter for the Dodgers against New York in 1948?

A. Rex Barney.

―――∞∞∞―――

Q. Now buried on the Ak-Sar-Ben grounds in Omaha, what horse was the winner of the Triple Crown in 1935?

A. Omaha.

―――∞∞∞―――

Q. What University of Nebraska halfback/defensive back of the 1930s was known as "the Wild Hoss of the Plains"?

A. Lloyd Cardwell.

―――∞∞∞―――

Q. What boxer from Omaha Tech won the 1939 national Golden Gloves title and earned a place on an Olympic team?

A. Carl Vinciquerra.

―――∞∞∞―――

Q. What former McCook resident has been chancellor of the University of Kansas and president of baseball's American League?

A. Gene Budig.

―――∞∞∞―――

Q. In 1972 what boxer fought Joe Frazier for the heavyweight championship in Omaha?

A. Ron Stander.

Q. What Omaha boxer fought nearly three hundred fights in the 1990s, was knocked out in five continents, and had a movie made about him?

A. Bruce "the Mouse" Strauss.

Q. Running for Jamaica, what former University of Nebraska sprinter won silver medals in the women's 10-meter and 200-meter dashes at the 1996 Olympics in Atlanta?

A. Merlene Ottey.

Q. What two former University of Nebraska running backs played in the same backfield with the San Francisco 49ers?

A. Roger Craig and Tom Rathman.

Q. In 1984 what University of Nebraska wide receiver was the number one draft choice by New England?

A. Irving Fryar.

Q. What World War I ace fighter pilot was the best known racecar driver in Omaha before the war?

A. Eddie Rickenbacker.

Q. Johnny Rodgers, the 1972 Heisman Trophy winner, played what positions for the Cornhuskers?

A. Running back and wide receiver.

Q. What Nebraska I-back won the Heisman Trophy in 1983?

A. Mike Rozier.

Q. When did Nebraska coach Bob Devaney win the Coach of the Year award of the Football Writers Association of America?

A. 1971.

Q. What horse owned by Omaha sportsman Michael Ford won the Kentucky Derby in 1966?

A. Kauai King.

Q. What former University of Nebraska basketball guard was killed in a plane crash in 1984?

A. Jack Moore.

Q. When the small plane he was piloting crashed in 1996, what University of Nebraska quarterback was killed?

A. Brook Berringer.

Q. What player for the Kansas City-Omaha Kings won the National Basketball Association scoring title in 1973?

A. Nate Archibald.

Q. What guard who played several years with the Omaha Racers was the NBA three-point shooting leader for the Washington Bullets in 1995–96?

A. Tim Legler.

Q. Who was the coach when Nebraska's basketball team won the National Invitation Tournament in 1996?

A. Danny Nee.

Q. What organizer of Omaha sporting events, who was a basketball star in the Olympics and is in the Naismith Memorial Basketball Hall of Fame, now coaches the Detroit Shocks in the Women's NBA?

A. Nancy Lieberman-Cline.

Q. What resident of Saint Paul, Nebraska, won 373 National League games and pitched 90 shutouts?

A. Grover Cleveland Alexander.

Q. Where was five-time American League batting champion Wade Boggs born?

A. Omaha.

Q. With what team did three-time American League batting champion George Brett play before moving up to the Kansas City Royals?

A. Omaha Royals.

Q. What All-Star Boston Celtic guard coached the Kansas City-Omaha Kings in the National Basketball Association?

A. Bob Cousy.

Q. At the age of seventeen, hockey immortal Gordie Howe played for what team before moving up to the Detroit Red Wings?

A. Omaha Knights.

Q. What NBA All-Star center coached the Creighton University basketball team?

A. Willis Reed.

Q. What graduate of Omaha Central High School twice led the National Football League in rushing?

A. Gale Sayers.

———⚬⚬⚬———

Q. What National League Most Valuable Player played third base with the Class A Omaha Cardinals?

A. Ken Boyer.

———⚬⚬⚬———

Q. What 1965 pitcher for the University of Nebraska won the American League Rookie of the Year award in 1968 with the Yankees?

A. Stan Bahnsen.

———⚬⚬⚬———

Q. How many touchdowns did Cornhusker I-back Lawrence Phillips score in the 1996 Fiesta Bowl?

A. Three.

———⚬⚬⚬———

Q. What Baltimore pitcher from Omaha's Northwest High School was Rookie of the Year in 1989?

A. Gregg Olson.

———⚬⚬⚬———

Q. What three participants in the 1997 World Series once played for the Omaha Royals?

A. Jeff Conine, Jim Eisenreich, and Kevin Seitzer.

———⚬⚬⚬———

Q. What was the hometown of Bud Tinning, who pitched for the Chicago Cubs against the Yankees in the 1932 World Series?

A. Pilger.

Q. Including the British Open in 1989, what native of Laurel has won nine golf tournaments on the PGA Tour?

A. Mark Calcavecchia.

Q. What was the first exclusively collegiate venue to install instant replay boards for its football fans?

A. Nebraska's Memorial Stadium.

Q. In 1981 and 1982 what graduate of Omaha's South High School won football's Outland Trophies at the University of Nebraska?

A. Dave Rimington.

Q. What former University of Nebraska football player is head coach at the University of Wisconsin?

A. Barry Alvarez.

Q. What former assistant of Nebraska football coach Bob Devaney coached the University of Missouri?

A. Warren Powers.

Q. Who was Bob Devaney's immediate predecessor as coach at the University of Nebraska?

A. Bill Jennings.

Q. What team was defeated, 35–31, by Nebraska in the 1971 "Game of the Century"?

A. Oklahoma.

Q. Where did Nebraska coach Bob Devaney play collegiate football?

A. Alma College.

———∞———

Q. When did four Texas colleges join the Big Eight to make it the Big Twelve?

A. 1994.

———∞———

Q. What former Nebraska football player was a five-time Pro Bowl performer with the Kansas City Chiefs and played in the 1998 Super Bowl for the champion Denver Broncos?

A. Neil Smith.

———∞———

Q. What assistant football coach at the University of Nebraska has written two books with Christian inspirational messages?

A. Ron Brown.

———∞———

Q. What Omaha insurance executive was Nebraska handball doubles champion seven times?

A. Jim Gabrielson.

———∞———

Q. What ex-Cornhusker set National Football League records in kickoff and punt returns with the New Orleans Saints?

A. Tyrone Hughes.

———∞———

Q. What former Nebraska offensive lineman was named the Kansas City Chief's Rookie of the Year in 1993?

A. Will Shields.

Q. What former Nebraska defensive back made twenty-seven interceptions in nine years with Cleveland, the New York Jets, and Kansas City Chiefs?

A. Brian Washington.

Q. Who was coach of the University of Nebraska 1997 women's gymnastic Big Twelve champions?

A. Dan Kendig.

Q. What long-time KFAB sports announcer greeted sensational plays with a shout of "man, woman, and child"?

A. Lyell Bremser.

Q. Who was the first Cornhusker to earn first-team All-America honors in women's soccer?

A. Kari Uppinghouse.

Q. When the Nebraska Memorial Stadium record attendance of 76,663 was set in 1987, who was the opponent?

A. Oklahoma.

Q. What years did Nebraska coach Bob Devaney win back-to-back national football championships?

A. 1970 and 1971.

Q. What star Nebraska quarterback was sidelined during much of the 1994 national championship season with a blood clot behind his right knee?

A. Tommy Frazier.

Q. In 1995 who broke the Nebraska record in rushing for freshmen with 1,086 yards?

A. Ahman Green.

———— ∞ ————

Q. What University of Nebraska at Omaha faculty member once coached the Afghan national basketball team?

A. Tom Gouttierre.

———— ∞ ————

Q. Where are the Cornhusker State Games that draw eighteen to twenty thousand athletes held each summer?

A. Lincoln.

———— ∞ ————

Q. Who is the first woman to be a director of football operations at the University of Nebraska and first at any NCAA Division I university?

A. Pat Logsdon.

———— ∞ ————

Q. Despite his deafness, what Nebraska defensive lineman played for the Denver Broncos?

A. Kenny Walker.

———— ∞ ————

Q. What team selected Nebraska's Rich King in the first round of the National Basketball Association draft?

A. Seattle Supersonics.

———— ∞ ————

Q. What former University of Nebraska quarterback, who played in the Canadian Football League, is on the Cornhusker coaching staff?

A. Turner Gill.

Q. Of the thousands of athletes who played in the first half century of the College World Series in Omaha, who was the top all-time position player selected in a 1996 vote?

A. Barry Bonds.

Q. Cornhusker running backs Ahman Green, Keith Jones, Calvin Jones, Joe Orduna, Leodis Flowers, and Jay Sims all attended what high school?

A. Omaha Central.

Q. What pitcher from Fairbury won twenty-five games for the Chicago Cubs over a five year career?

A. Doyle Lade.

Q. What Minnesota Vikings center played for Nebraska?

A. Mick Tingelhoff.

Q. What former Creighton University baseball coach won the College World Series in 1994 with his Oklahoma ball club?

A. Larry Cochell.

Q. Where did 1950 Nebraska All-American running back Bobby Reynolds play in high school?

A. Grand Island.

Q. What Nebraska quarterback completed 145 passes in 1976, the most ever by a Cornhusker in one season?

A. Vince Ferragamo.

Q. What Southern California coach was selected by fans in 1996 as coach of the all-time team of the College World Series, which has been played in Omaha for fifty years?

A. Rod Dedeaux.

Q. What University of Nebraska All-American was the setter on the U.S. women's volleyball team that won bronze in the 1992 Olympics?

A. Lori Endicott.

Q. What National Basketball Association coach was the baseball coach for Creighton University for three seasons?

A. Bill Fitch.

Q. Who holds the Cornhusker record of 294 yards rushing in a single game?

A. Calvin Jones.

Q. What was the hometown of Buford Bailey, all-around champion of the Grand American Trapshoot?

A. Big Springs.

Q. Who holds the Nebraska basketball record for most points scored in a game with forty-two?

A. Eric Piatkowski.

Q. In 1949–50, when Nebraska shared the crown with Kansas and Kansas State, who led the Big Seven conference in scoring?

A. Claude Retherford.

Q. How many touchdowns did Cornhusker Johnny Rodgers score in the 1973 Orange Bowl?

A. Four.

Q. Who was a Big Six and Big Ten referee after playing halfback for the University of Nebraska from 1938 to 1940?

A. Herman Rohrig.

Q. In the 1971 "Game of the Century" in which Nebraska defeated Oklahoma, what quarterback was voted Most Valuable Player?

A. Jerry Tagge.

Q. In what event did Nebraska fullback Sam Francis compete in the 1936 Olympics?

A. Shot put.

Q. As the star quarterback at Hastings College who was named College Athlete of the Year in 1959 by the *Omaha World-Herald*?

A. Tom Osborne.

Q. Who coached the Nebraska Rose Bowl team of 1941?

A. Biff Jones.

Q. From what source did the money come to pay for the Devaney Sports Center in Lincoln?

A. Cigarette tax.

Q. Who was hired as Nebraska's first full-time coach—for both football and basketball—in 1911?

A. E. O. "Jumbo" Stiehm.

———— ∞ ————

Q. In 1950 what six-foot, ten-inch center from Scottsbluff was the first Cornhusker selected to play in the East-West All Star Game?

A. Milton "Bus" Whitehead.

———— ∞ ————

Q. What former University of Nebraska volleyball player was a two-time All-American and has been a Nebraska assistant coach for nine years?

A. Cathy Noth.

———— ∞ ————

Q. When was D. X. Bible football coach at the University of Nebraska?

A. 1929–36.

———— ∞ ————

Q. Coach Tom Osborne won his 250th victory by trampling old rival Oklahoma, 69–7, on what date?

A. November 1, 1997.

———— ∞ ————

Q. Who holds the all-time career record of 4,780 rushing yards at the University of Nebraska?

A. Mike Rozier.

———— ∞ ————

Q. What Jackson State running back scored six touchdowns against the University of Nebraska at Omaha in 1974 during a 75–0 trouncing?

A. Walter Payton.

Q. Where did Danny Nee coach before taking over the basketball reins at the University of Nebraska in 1986?

A. Ohio University.

———— ∞∞ ————

Q. How many All-American basketball players have played for Nebraska since 1950?

A. Three (James Buchanan, Carl McPipe, and Dave Hoppen).

———— ∞∞ ————

Q. What University of Nebraska quarterback was state shot-put champion while in high school?

A. Scott Frost.

———— ∞∞ ————

Q. Who is the women's basketball coach at the University of Nebraska?

A. Paul Sanderford.

———— ∞∞ ————

Q. What were the names of the two University of Nebraska basketball guards who were All Big Six in 1941?

A. Sid Held and Don Fitz.

———— ∞∞ ————

Q. What position did Cornhusker I-back Jeff Kinney of "Game of the Century" fame play in high school?

A. Quarterback.

———— ∞∞ ————

Q. With twenty-four hundred teams, what Nebraska city has been called "the softball capital of the world"?

A. Omaha.

Q. What twelve-mile, hard-surface trail is the most popular for roller-blading in Omaha?

A. Keystone.

———— ∞ ————

Q. What player who scored a Nebraska touchdown in the 1941 Rose Bowl had a long career as head coach at Kearney State?

A. Al Zikmund.

———— ∞ ————

Q. How many athletes turn out for the Nebraska Special Olympics summer games in Omaha each year?

A. Around fifteen hundred.

———— ∞ ————

Q. What is the second largest corporate road race in the nation?

A. Omaha Corporate Cup Run.

———— ∞ ————

Q. What two 1980 Olympic gold medal gymnasts trained in their early years at Omaha's Sokol Hall?

A. Phil Cahoy and Jim Hartung.

———— ∞ ————

Q. What National League strikeout king from Nebraska once played basketball with the Harlem Globe Trotters?

A. Bob Gibson.

———— ∞ ————

Q. What Nebraska quarterback passed for over one thousand yards and rushed for over one thousand yards the same season?

A. Scott Frost.

Q. Palmyra was the home of what 1980 Olympics volleyball star?

A. Julie Vollertsen.

Q. Who has been head basketball coach at Creighton, Arkansas, Kentucky, and Oklahoma State?

A. Eddie Sutton.

Q. Derek Brown and Calvin Jones shared the I-back position for the Cornhuskers so effectively in 1991–92 that they were known by what name?

A. We-backs.

Q. In what year did the Creighton University men's soccer team post its best record, making it to the NCAA Final Four?

A. 1996.

Q. What six-man high school football team won the state championship in 1997 after one of its members drowned in the Platte River?

A. Benedict.

Q. What Millard North High School graduate, swimming for Creighton University, won the 100-yard butterfly in the National Catholic Swimming Meet in 1989?

A. Matt Gabrielson.

Q. What former governor of Nebraska played tennis in Lincoln into his eighties?

A. Robert Crosby.

Q. Who was the grand old man of Omaha tennis, who played a competitive game until he was nearly ninety years old?

A. Fletcher "Duke" Slater.

Q. The Creighton University baseball team made it to the College World Series in what year?

A. 1991.

Q. In 1996 what women's volleyball team won the national championship in NCAA Division II?

A. UNO Lady Mavs.

Q. What sophomore I-back, who began as a walk-on, piled up 1,201 yards in 1978, second best for Nebraska at that time?

A. I. M. Hipp.

Q. What Nebraska college baseball team won the National Association of Intercollegiate Athletics World Series in 1995?

A. Bellevue University.

Q. What brothers who starred in basketball at the University of Nebraska at Omaha later played together for the Omaha Racers professional team?

A. Dean and Tommy Thompson.

Q. To what political office was former Nebraska tight end Jim McFarland elected?

A. State senator.

Q. What team won the North Central Conference football championship in 1996?

A. UNO Mavericks.

Q. What Cornhusker running back out-gained Barry Sanders, 256 yards to 189, in a game with Oklahoma State in 1988?

A. Ken Clark.

Q. What are the names of Nebraska's two amateur ice hockey teams?

A. Omaha Lancers and Lincoln Stars.

Q. What percentage of the University of Nebraska football players receive degrees?

A. 63 percent.

Q. Who was the first UNO volleyball player to earn All-America honors as a freshman?

A. Tracy Ankeny.

Q. In what year did Nebraska's baseball team, coached by John Sanders, begin the season with twenty-seven straight wins?

A. 1983.

Q. What Cornhusker quarterback broke seven tackles in a seventy-five-yard touchdown run during a 62-24 blowout of Florida in the 1996 Fiesta Bowl?

A. Tommy Frazier.

Q. Where will the 1999 National Junior Olympic Track and Field Championships be held?

A. Omaha's Burke Stadium.

Q. How many Nebraska football players were named to the 1997 Associated Press All-America first team?

A. Three (Aaron Taylor, Grant Wistrom, and Jason Peter).

Q. What Omaha grocery store owner holds the University of Iowa record for tackles with 492?

A. Larry Station.

Q. What Nebraska running back's Heisman Trophy chances in 1980 were ruined by injuries?

A. Jarvis Redwine.

Q. In 1981 what Cornhusker running back rolled up 234 yards—including a 94-yard touchdown run—against Florida State?

A. Roger Craig.

Q. What outfielder from Nelson played in the majors for twelve years, with his best year being 1966 at Baltimore when he batted .306?

A. Russ Snyder.

Q. What former 160-pound Nebraska fullback succeeded Tom Osborne as Cornhusker coach?

A. Frank Solich.

Q. In 1967 who scored more points (fifty-one) in a single game than any other Creighton University basketball player in history?

A. Bob Portman.

Q. What was the weight of Tom "Train Wreck" Novak, a four-time all-conference selection who played center, fullback, and linebacker for Nebraska during 1946–49?

A. 205 pounds.

Q. With 1,882 points, who was the third highest career scorer in Nebraska basketball history?

A. Jerry Fort.

Q. In 1997 what Creighton University senior won the Hermann Trophy given to the nation's best collegiate soccer player?

A. Johnny Torres.

Q. Who was the only Cornhusker fullback to rush for over two hundred yards (204) in one game?

A. Frank Solich in 1965.

Q. Frank Leahy, former Notre Dame football player and coach, lived in what two Nebraska towns?

A. O'Neill and Omaha.

Q. Where is the National Museum of Roller Skating?

A. Lincoln.

Q. What Scottsbluff Junior College football player became a star with the Detroit Lions?

A. Dick "Night Train" Lane.

Q. What Beemer-born and Omaha-raised pitcher won 223 games in the major leagues over twenty years, all with Cleveland?

A. Mel Harder.

Q. What Hall of Fame pitcher and winner of 197 games attended school in Hastings?

A. Dazzy Vance.

Q. How many yards did Nebraska's Ahman Green gain when setting the Orange Bowl rushing record in 1998?

A. 206.

Q. George Halas called what Nebraska player from Blue Springs "the greatest two-way end of all time"?

A. Guy Chamberlin.

Q. Who scored the touchdown in the closing moments of the 1970 Orange Bowl game that gave Nebraska the national title?

A. Jerry Tagge.

Q. With the fabled Four Horsemen playing, Notre Dame won thirty games and lost only two, both to what team?

A. Nebraska, in 1922 and 1923.

Q. Knute Rockne thought which Cornhusker from Superior was "the best tackle (he had) ever seen"?

A. Ed Weir.

Q. In what year did infielder Nellie Fox and pitcher Bobby Shantz, two future big-league stars, play with the Lincoln Chiefs?

A. 1948.

Q. What Nebraskan scored the first touchdown in the 1941 Rose Bowl game with Stanford?

A. Vike Francis.

Q. What 1949 All-American back from Omaha University played seven years with the San Francisco 49ers as a kick returner?

A. Joe Arenas.

Q. After reaching the National Football League, what Omaha University quarterback was converted into a defensive back and wide receiver and played for the undefeated Miami Dolphins of 1972?

A. Marlin Briscoe.

Q. Before moving to Creighton University, what native of Wilber coached the Kansas State basketball team?

A. Dana Altman.

Q. With what team did Chadron State's pass-catching Don Beebe play in the 1997 Super Bowl?

A. Green Bay.

Q. What Dallas Cowboys tight end who played college ball for Wyoming was originally from Gothenburg?

A. Jay Novacek.

Q. What is the name of the golf course near Mullen that was designed by Bill Coore and Masters champion Ben Crenshaw?

A. Sandhills Golf Club.

Q. In 1931 what famous pilot was killed in a plane race at the Omaha Municipal Airport before fifteen thousand fans?

A. Charles W. "Speed" Holman.

Q. What Creighton University basketball star went on to set rebounding records in the NBA?

A. Paul Silas.

Q. At what course did Robert Mitera make golf's longest hole in one, a 444-yard drive?

A. Miracle Hills, Omaha.

Q. When did the Cornhusker basketball team upset Kansas University, 43–41, with Wilt Chamberlain as the Kansas center?

A. February 22, 1958.

Q. What Nebraska basketball coach finished with 253 victories, about one-fourth of the team's all-time total at that time?

A. Joe Cipriano.

Q. On average, how many people attend the weekly NASCAR-sanctioned auto races at Omaha's Sunset Speedway?

A. Four thousand.

Q. Before sports writer Cy Sherman gave them their present name in 1902, what school's football teams were known as the Bug Eaters, Golden Knights, and Antelopes?

A. Nebraska Cornhuskers.

Q. Where was the first game of six-man football played, a game invented by Stephen Epler in 1934?

A. Chester.

Q. What was the last name of Joe, Emil, Rudy, and Ernie, Omaha brothers who were dominant figures on the midwestern wrestling scene?

A. Dusek.

Q. Who was the marksman from Axtell who won gold medals in three position free rifle shooting in the 1964 and 1968 Olympics?

A. Gary Anderson.

Q. What University of Nebraska sophomore bowled three consecutive three hundred games in the Junior Cornhusker Tournament at Sun Valley Lanes on February 2, 1997, in Lincoln?

A. Jeremy Sonnenfeld.

Q. With 2,167 points, the all-time basketball scoring leader at the University of Nebraska was what Omaha Benson High School graduate?

A. Dave Hoppen.

Q. What University of Nebraska sprinter from North Platte once held the world record in the 200-meter dash?

A. Roland Locke.

Q. What Omaha Bryan High School graduate and Army marksmanship specialist won the world air-rifle championship at Munich in 1998?

A. Jason Parker.

Q. What organization in Omaha promotes tournaments each summer for three-player basketball?

A. Hoop-It-Up.

Q. What former Ralston softball pitcher is considered the toughest woman arm wrestler in the nation?

A. Mary McConnaughey.

Q. What former executive editor of the *Omaha World-Herald* was also a city, state, and regional men's tennis champion?

A. Lou Gerdes.

Q. Where was the Log Rolling (Birling) National Championship held on September 9, 1898?

A. Omaha.

Q. What former Creighton University baseball player was the *Sporting News* National League Rookie Pitcher of the Year in 1996 with a 13–10 record at St. Louis?

A. Alan Benes.

Q. What town was the home of Joe Stecher, world champion wrestler from 1915 to 1919 and from 1920 to 1926?

A. Dodge.

Q. Who was the Creighton University basketball guard of the post World War II era who became Douglas County Attorney?

A. Pinky Knowles.

Q. What native of Plattsmouth, owner of the *Hastings Tribune* and a big game hunter, donated one of the world's largest collection of African animals to the Nebraska State Museum?

A. Adam Beede.

Q. What pair of All-American defensive linemen on the 1997 University of Nebraska championship football team wrote a book called *Heart and Soul*?

A. Jason Peter and Grant Wistrom.

Q. What mayor of Omaha played in the outfield for the Omaha Packers in the old Class A Western League in the 1930s?

A. Johnny Rosenblatt.

Q. In 1927, what future president of the Omaha Printing Company pitched batting practice against Babe Ruth in Omaha?

A. Bill Bloom.

Q. What graduate of Omaha Northwest High School became the U.S. light cruiserweight, Thai kick-boxing champion in 1998?

A. Kurt Podany.

SCIENCE & NATURE

C H A P T E R S I X

Q. Where is the Union Pacific's high-tech Harriman Dispatch Center, which controls all its trains?

A. Omaha.

Q. How much did the Nebraska record blue catfish weigh that was caught in the Missouri River near Wynot in 1970 by Raynold Promes?

A. One hundred pounds, eight ounces.

Q. Where were the *Enola Gay* and the *Bocks Car,* the B-29s that dropped atomic bombs on Japan, assembled?

A. Glenn Martin plant, Bellevue.

Q. The world's busiest railroad switching yard is the Union Pacific's Edd Bailey facility in what city?

A. North Platte.

Q. What Nebraska native invented the center pivot irrigation system?

A. Frank Zybach.

Q. What president of the University of Chicago who won the Nobel Prize in 1958 for physiology/medicine was born in Wahoo?

A. George W. Beadle.

Q. How big was the world-record wild turkey shot by Tim Jones with bow and arrow near Plattsmouth on April 23, 1996?

A. 33.85 pounds.

Q. The world population of whooping cranes, which rest along the Platte River on their flights to their nesting grounds, reached a low of fifteen birds in what year?

A. 1941.

Q. When was ground broken for the $31 million George W. Beadle Center for Genetics and Biomaterials Research at the University of Nebraska?

A. 1992.

Q. During World War I, what present-day ghost town was the center of Nebraska's potash industry in the Sand Hills?

A. Antioch.

Q. Where were most of the nation's military balloonists trained during World War I?

A. Fort Omaha.

Q. Where are Nebraska's two nuclear energy plants?

A. Fort Calhoun and Brownville.

Q. What nickname has been given to Nebraska's burrowing owl because of its constant head bobbing?

A. "Howdy Owl."

Q. What scientist became chancellor of the University of Nebraska in 1946?

A. Reuben Gustavson.

Q. Where is the largest tract of virgin timber in Nebraska?

A. Fontenelle Forest, near Bellevue.

Q. When were pheasants first imported into Nebraska?

A. 1915.

Q. The first telegraph line into the Nebraska Territory was strung in 1860 from Saint Joseph, Missouri, to what town?

A. Brownville.

Q. Who brought the first steamboat, the *Western Engineer,* up the Missouri River to Fort Lisa past the present site of Omaha in 1819?

A. Maj. Stephen H. Long.

Q. Bobcats have expanded from their traditional range in north-west Nebraska to what area?

A. South of the Platte.

Q. When was the first telephone set up in Nebraska at Omaha?

A. 1877.

———⊗⊗⊗———

Q. What scientist at the University of Nebraska was instrumental in developing its agricultural experiment station?

A. Charles Bessey.

———⊗⊗⊗———

Q. What physical disorder is the target of the Boys Town National Research Hospital in Omaha?

A. Deafness.

———⊗⊗⊗———

Q. What is the only insect in Nebraska on the federal threatened or endangered list?

A. American burying beetle.

———⊗⊗⊗———

Q. The new Peter Kiewit Institute of Information Science and the First Data Resources Building are both on the former site of what Omaha racetrack?

A. Ak-Sar-Ben.

———⊗⊗⊗———

Q. How much did the Nebraska record paddlefish weigh that was caught by Warren Yelkin at Gavins Point Dam in 1978?

A. Sixty-one pounds, eight ounces.

———⊗⊗⊗———

Q. The high-tech U.S. Strategic Command headquarters is based at what former cavalry outpost near Omaha?

A. Fort Crook.

Q. What is the weight of the trumpeter swans that can be seen along the Platte River from time to time?

A. Around thirty pounds.

———— ∞∞ ————

Q. Cargill has built facilities worth $425 million in Blair to process what grain?

A. Corn.

———— ∞∞ ————

Q. What poisonous spiders are found in Nebraska?

A. Black widow and brown recluse.

———— ∞∞ ————

Q. What is the Nebraska state bird?

A. Western meadowlark.

———— ∞∞ ————

Q. What Nebraskan who lived in Fremont and Aurora invented the modern stroboscope?

A. Harold "Doc" Edgerton.

———— ∞∞ ————

Q. What is the average annual rainfall in Omaha?

A. Thirty inches.

———— ∞∞ ————

Q. What is the average annual snowfall in Omaha?

A. Twenty-two inches.

Q. In the winter what westerly winds sometimes warm north-western Nebraska?

A. Chinook.

―――∞∞∞―――

Q. What is the nation's largest hand-planted forest, which is in Thomas County?

A. Nebraska National Forest (98,000 acres).

―――∞∞∞―――

Q. What brothers built the telegraph lines that linked the continent and also founded a university in Omaha?

A. Edward and John A. Creighton.

―――∞∞∞―――

Q. Where is the eagle-viewing facility built by the Central Nebraska Public Power and Irrigation District in 1996?

A. Lake Ogallala.

―――∞∞∞―――

Q. What doctor stationed at Fort Robinson, Fort Omaha, and Fort Sidney later gained fame fighting yellow fever in Cuba?

A. Walter Reed.

―――∞∞∞―――

Q. What weather event was called "the School Children's Storm" because it caught so many of them away from home?

A. Blizzard of 1888.

―――∞∞∞―――

Q. What resident of Ord was Nebraska's best-known aviatrix and the nation's first female pilot?

A. Evelyn Genevieve Sharp.

Q. What birds that nest on Platte River sandbars have suffered from the erratic water flows caused by irrigation?

A. Least terns and piping plovers.

———— ∞∞ ————

Q. Who was the first white man to discover the Agate Fossil Beds, thirty-four miles north of Mitchell?

A. Capt. James H. Cook.

———— ∞∞ ————

Q. What is the top speed of the pronghorn antelope, which number around six thousand in Nebraska?

A. Sixty miles per hour.

———— ∞∞ ————

Q. On October 10, 1960, where did the first manned flight of a modern hot air balloon take place?

A. Bruning.

———— ∞∞ ————

Q. Where is the world's best-known tractor-testing laboratory?

A. Lincoln.

———— ∞∞ ————

Q. Among the fifty states, where did Nebraska place in completing its segment of the Interstate Highway system?

A. First.

———— ∞∞ ————

Q. What plant was declared the official state flower in 1895?

A. Goldenrod.

Q. In 1972 what tree replaced the American elm as the official state tree?

A. Cottonwood.

Q. What is the official state mammal?

A. White-tailed deer.

Q. What became the official state insect in 1974 as the result of a suggestion by Auburn school children?

A. Honeybee.

Q. What was the highest temperature recorded in Nebraska?

A. 118 degrees Fahrenheit (Geneva in 1934, Hartington in 1936, and Minden in 1936).

Q. What was the coldest temperature recorded in Nebraska?

A. Minus 47 degrees Fahrenheit (Camp Clarke in 1899 and Oshkosh in 1989).

Q. Where was the Vise-Grip wrench invented?

A. DeWitt.

Q. Where was an unsuccessful attempt made in 1860 to combine a covered wagon and a steam engine into one vehicle?

A. Nebraska City.

Q. How many deer were killed in collisions with motor vehicles in 1995?

A. Around five thousand (4,976).

──── ⊗⊗⊗ ────

Q. What Nebraska City resident founded the Morton Salt Company?

A. Joy Morton.

──── ⊗⊗⊗ ────

Q. In the late 1980s what was the average number of squirrels killed by all Nebraska hunters per year?

A. Ninety-three thousand.

──── ⊗⊗⊗ ────

Q. What was the formal name of the four planes, known as the "Flying White House," that stood ready at Omaha's Offutt Air Force Base to fly the president if nuclear war broke out?

A. National Airborne Operations Center.

──── ⊗⊗⊗ ────

Q. What minesweeper is on exhibit near the Missouri River in Omaha?

A. USS *Hazard*.

──── ⊗⊗⊗ ────

Q. Where did the Missouri River change its course, leaving a bridge over dry land?

A. Decatur.

──── ⊗⊗⊗ ────

Q. One of the most outstanding fossilized flowers in existence was discovered in the brick works of what town?

A. Endicott.

Q. Where is Nebraska's largest fish hatchery?

A. Calamus Reservoir, near Burwell.

Q. What town was the hub of the western Nebraska intercontinental ballistic missile sites during the cold war?

A. Kimball.

Q. Where is the state's only railroad tunnel, built in 1888 but now closed?

A. Near Belmont.

Q. What University of Nebraska professor has been called "the Father of American Parasitology"?

A. Henry Baldwin Ward.

Q. How many University of Nebraska students died from Spanish influenza in 1918?

A. Eighty-five.

Q. What University of Nebraska professor invented the random-access magnetic core memory, a key component of computers?

A. Jay Forrester.

Q. What famed inventor came to Omaha in 1898 to supervise the lighting at the Grand Court of the Trans Mississippi Exposition?

A. Thomas A. Edison.

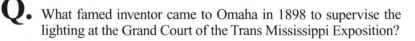

Q. What four-foot-tall birds, numbering approximately half a million, spend six weeks each year along the Platte River?

A. Sandhill cranes.

Q. When did the National Science Foundation select University of Nebraska as the site for the Center of Mass Spectrometry (analysis of fine molecules)?

A. 1978.

Q. In 1987 Donald Cram of the University of Nebraska shared the Nobel Prize in what discipline?

A. Chemistry.

Q. What UNL alumnus was the co-discoverer of the most distant known quasar?

A. Donald Schneider.

Q. The Great Plains Regional Center for Environmental Change was established at UNL to conduct research on what subject?

A. Global warming.

Q. In 1898 who was the first woman graduate to complete all of her medical school training at Creighton University?

A. Anna Marie Griffith.

Q. What Creighton Medical School faculty member gained a national reputation in cancer research?

A. Dr. Henry Lynch.

Q. What credit card processing company has sixty-five hundred employees in Omaha?

A. First Data Resources.

Q. What Creighton University professor was co-author of *Strength Training Past 50*?

A. Tom Baechle.

Q. Who caught the Nebraska record brown trout weighing twenty pounds, one ounce, in the Snake River in 1973?

A. Denny Doolittle.

Q. Operation of the six big dams on the upper Missouri River is controlled by the U.S. Army Corps of Engineers in what city?

A. Omaha.

Q. What chairman of the Creighton University Art Department set up a program to monitor Russian television broadcasts?

A. Rev. Lee Lubbers.

Q. How long is the growing season for southeast Nebraska?

A. 170 days.

Q. When was the Trident submarine USS *Nebraska* commissioned?

A. 1993.

Q. On what Omaha campus can the prestigious Eppley Institute for Research in Cancer & Allied Diseases be found?

A. University of Nebraska Medical Center.

———— ∞∞∞ ————

Q. What record-setting aviator learned to fly at the Lincoln Airplane and Flying School in the 1920s when Lincoln was an important airplane manufacturing center?

A. Charles A. Lindbergh.

———— ∞∞∞ ————

Q. How much remains of the original wetlands in the 4,200-square-mile Rainwater Basin in south central Nebraska?

A. Less than 10 percent.

———— ∞∞∞ ————

Q. What Overton-born surgeon became assistant secretary of health in the Department of Health, Education, and Welfare?

A. Charles C. Edwards.

———— ∞∞∞ ————

Q. What market researcher and public opinion analyst was born in Hebron?

A. Elmo Roper.

———— ∞∞∞ ————

Q. Where does the liver transplant program of the University of Nebraska rank with those of other medical schools?

A. Top five.

———— ∞∞∞ ————

Q. Where in Omaha can diners look through picture windows at wild raccoons cavorting?

A. Alpine Inn.

Q. Who created the Henry Doorly Zoo's spectacular Lied Jungle and its innovative Scott Aquarium in Omaha?

A. Lee Simmons.

———⊗⊗⊗———

Q. In 1976 what native Omahan was chosen Outstanding Psychiatrist in the Nation?

A. Dr. Frank Menolascino.

———⊗⊗⊗———

Q. What Omahan won the 1980 Nobel Prize for economics?

A. Lawrence Klein.

———⊗⊗⊗———

Q. What name has been given to the seventy-five-acre educational display of foliage and flowers taking shape in South Omaha?

A. Omaha Botanical Gardens.

———⊗⊗⊗———

Q. What is the smallest city in the United States with two medical schools?

A. Omaha.

———⊗⊗⊗———

Q. Who was a founder and the first president of Omaha-based First Data Corporation, which processes one out of three credit card transactions in the nation?

A. P. E. "Bill" Esping.

———⊗⊗⊗———

Q. L. Ron Hubbard, founder of the Church of Scientology, was born in what town?

A. Tilden.

Q. As of March 1997, how many kidney transplants had been performed at Clarkson Hospital/UNMC in Omaha?

A. 1,062.

Q. What physicist from Merriman won the Nobel Prize in 1980?

A. Val L. Fitch.

Q. Where do college students stage races with laboratory rats in an event known as "the Rat Olympics"?

A. Nebraska Wesleyan University.

Q. What Omaha businessman, who once sang with Charlie Barnet's band, has spent more than $9 million for advertisements fighting cholesterol?

A. Phil Sokolof.

Q. University of Nebraska physicists Greg Snow and Dan Claeswill are building a device to be used with the new $6 billion particle accelerator in what European city?

A. Geneva.

Q. How much will Sprint spend to convert its western Nebraska and eastern Wyoming telephone system to an all-digital network?

A. $45 million.

Q. On what thirty-story Omaha building were attempts made in the 1990s to raise peregrine falcons?

A. Woodmen Tower.

Q. What sandwich did the University of Nebraska College of Agriculture develop for McDonald's?

A. McRibs.

Q. Where was Nebraska's first nuclear power plant, now no longer in operation?

A. Hallam.

Q. While Arbor Day founder J. Sterling Morton was making speeches, who did most of the tree planting at Arbor Lodge in Nebraska City?

A. His wife and children.

Q. At what hour on the first Saturday of each month are Omaha's Civil Defense sirens tested?

A. 10:00 A.M.

Q. After he suffered a mild heart attack, what CEO of ConAgra developed its popular Healthy Choice brand of food?

A. Charles M. "Mike" Harper.

Q. As of March 1997, how many bone marrow transplants had been undertaken by the University of Nebraska Medical Center?

A. 1,975.

Q. What is the hometown of Charles Purcell, designer of the Oakland-San Francisco Bay Bridge?

A. North Bend.

Q. Where is the University of Nebraska at Omaha leading the project to excavate an ancient lost city?

A. Bethsaida, Israel.

―――∞∞∞―――

Q. What fish is most popular with anglers in Nebraska?

A. Catfish.

―――∞∞∞―――

Q. Where is Ole's Big Game Steakhouse with its two hundred mounted trophies from all over the world?

A. Paxton.

―――∞∞∞―――

Q. What Sand Hills community of three hundred people is the site of Nebraska's newest airport?

A. Thedford.

―――∞∞∞―――

Q. What Union Pacific president and U.S. rubber czar began as a call boy summoning crews in the North Platte yards?

A. William Jeffers.

―――∞∞∞―――

Q. The burn center serving Nebraska and neighboring states is at what Lincoln hospital?

A. Saint Elizabeth.

―――∞∞∞―――

Q. What is the hometown of Thomas J. Hargrave, former president of the Eastman Kodak Company?

A. Wymore.

Q. In what county are most of the world's approximately one hundred surviving Salt Creek tiger beetles?

A. Saunders.

Q. What Millard North High School physics teacher received the $25,000 Milken Family Foundation National Educator Award in 1997?

A. Roger Kassebaum.

Q. How many Omaha Public Power District customers were without power, some for up to eleven days, after the snowstorm of October 26, 1997?

A. 150,000.

Q. What is the name of the first Indian woman, who practiced in Bancroft and Walthill, to earn a medical degree?

A. Dr. Susan La Flesche Picotte.

Q. Near what state park is the new $26 million Strategic Air Command Museum with all its planes parked indoors?

A. Mahoney.

Q. Where does Nebraska rank among the states in number of species of butterflies?

A. Tenth.

Q. What company at Valley is the world's largest producer of center pivot irrigation systems?

A. Valmont Industries.

Q. What huge underground reservoir of water exists under Nebraska and neighboring states?

A. Ogallala Aquifer.

Q. What University of Nebraska graduate once was chairman of Warner Lambert Company?

A. Joe Williams.

Q. How many flights per day are provided by Omaha's Eppley Airfield?

A. 180.

Q. What is the elevation of Omaha?

A. 997 feet above sea level.

Q. What company provides local telephone service for Omaha?

A. US West.

Q. How many students attend the University of Nebraska Medical Center in Omaha?

A. Twenty-seven hundred.

Q. What was the parent company of Inacom, a technology company with its headquarters in Omaha and revenues of $3.1 billion?

A. Valmont Industries.

Q. What immigrant from India founded American Business Information, a $190 million-a-year Omaha company, in his garage?

A. Vinod Gupta.

Q. What former Nebraska farm boy runs Omaha-based CalEnergy, which had $5.7 billion in assets in 1996?

A. David Sokol.

Q. What Denmark native is chief executive officer of Valmont Industries, the irrigation equipment manufacturer in Valley?

A. Mogens C. Bay.

Q. How many sets of triplets were born in Nebraska in 1996?

A. Twenty-one.

Q. What was the average age of women giving birth to their first child in Nebraska in 1996?

A. 24.4 years.

Q. Where is Kellogg's third most productive cereal plant, now undergoing a $100 million upgrading?

A. Omaha.

Q. Where can one find the James Arthur Vineyards, Nebraska's newest winery?

A. Between Raymond and Lincoln.

Q. Where do Nebraska farmers store their corn and soybeans when the railroads, elevators, and barges are full?

A. On the ground.

———⊗⊗⊗———

Q. What Omaha company played a leading role in building a $1.2 billion oil drilling platform off the coast of Newfoundland?

A. Peter Kiewit Sons' Inc.

———⊗⊗⊗———

Q. Where was Kool-Aid invented by Edwin Perkins in 1927?

A. Hastings.

———⊗⊗⊗———

Q. What company bought the Hudson Foods plant at Columbus after it closed in 1997 because of E. coli bacteria in its ground beef?

A. Iowa Beef Packers.

———⊗⊗⊗———

Q. What Omaha trucking firm has a backup headquarters in a 66,000 square foot building to control its trucks if its primary headquarters is destroyed?

A. Werner Enterprises.

———⊗⊗⊗———

Q. How many miles of fiber optics lines does US West have in Nebraska?

A. Thirty-four hundred.

———⊗⊗⊗———

Q. What graduate of Omaha's Benson High School is the top executive with US West Communications in Nebraska?

A. Rex Fisher.

Q. Where are the official National Weather Service temperature readings taken for Omaha?

A. Eppley Airfield.

Q. Where is the National Weather Service station for the greater Omaha area?

A. Valley.

Q. What is the windiest month of the year for Omaha, with an average of 12.7 miles per hour?

A. April.

Q. What percentage of the days are sunny in Omaha?

A. 60 percent.

Q. What was the record high temperature in Omaha set in July 1936?

A. 114 degrees Fahrenheit.

Q. What was the record low temperature in Omaha set in January 1884?

A. Minus 32 degrees Fahrenheit.

Q. Where in Omaha is the twenty-two-foot sculpture that was erected in 1975 to commemorate the killer tornado of that year?

A. Pipal Park.

Q. Big Boy, a steam locomotive, and Centennial, the largest diesel locomotive ever made, are on display in what park?

A. Kenefick, in Omaha.

―――∞∞∞―――

Q. Where is the Mallory Kountze Planetarium?

A. University of Nebraska at Omaha.

―――∞∞∞―――

Q. What organization furnishes natural gas to Omaha?

A. Metropolitan Utilities District.

―――∞∞∞―――

Q. What Columbus inventor and head of a company that makes metal frameless buildings was known as "the Corn Belt Edison"?

A. Walter Behlen.

―――∞∞∞―――

Q. Where is the 130-acre University of Nebraska Technology Park being built to serve as an incubator for young high-tech companies?

A. Northwest Lincoln.

―――∞∞∞―――

Q. As of 1997, how many wishes has the Make-A-Wish Foundation of Nebraska granted to children with life-threatening illnesses?

A. Seven hundred.

―――∞∞∞―――

Q. Where is the broom factory that in 1926 was the largest in the world with two hundred employees?

A. Deshler.

Q. What is the medical specialty of William Berndt, chancellor of the University of Nebraska Medical Center in Omaha?

A. Pharmacology.

―――✦―――

Q. What engineering company was headed by Charles Durham, for whom the University of Nebraska at Omaha Durham Science Center was named?

A. HDR Inc. (Henningson, Durham & Richardson).

―――✦―――

Q. The bald eagle population in Nebraska has been growing since the banning of what chemical?

A. DDT.

―――✦―――

Q. What is the only insect with the word *Nebraska* in its name?

A. Nebraska cone-headed katydid.

―――✦―――

Q. What plant attracts monarch butterflies to Nebraska because it contains a poison that they ingest to repel predators?

A. Milkweed.

―――✦―――

Q. What Lincoln ophthalmologist designed the plastic eye lens implants that helped make cataract surgery routine?

A. Aziz Y. Anis.

―――✦―――

Q. After World War I, what Omahan developed the idea for pilot parachutes?

A. Allen Cecil Scott.

Q. Where is the world's largest open air aviary?

A. Henry Doorly Zoo, Omaha.

Q. Where was the underground nerve center of the Strategic Air Command?

A. Offutt Air Force Base.

Q. What two counties in Nebraska are named after animals?

A. Antelope and Buffalo.

Q. What birds that stop in the Omaha area are so numerous that they sometimes disrupt radio signals as far away as Kansas City and Des Moines?

A. Snow geese.

Q. Between 1900 and the late 1960s the wetlands of Nebraska were reduced from ninety-four thousand acres to how many acres?

A. Thirty-four thousand.

Q. How many raccoons were taken annually in the 1980s by fur hunters and trappers in Nebraska?

A. Seventy-three thousand.

Q. In 1911 what brothers from Ewing flew an airplane they had built themselves?

A. Savidge.

Q. The eastern cottontail rabbit is found throughout Nebraska, but the desert cottontail occurs mostly in what section of the state?

A. Western.

Q. What are the two most significant deer in Nebraska?

A. White-tailed and mule.

Q. In 1996 firearm hunters killed 37,423, archers 4,471, and muzzleloaders 3,583 of what animal?

A. Deer.

Q. When was the first successful oil well drilled in the Panhandle?

A. 1949.

Q. What vocal, cunning mammal is Nebraska's dominant terrestrial predator?

A. Coyote.

Q. Who purchased 782 acres on the Platte River east of Kearney to create the Lillian Annette Rowe Wildlife Sanctuary?

A. National Audubon Society.

Q. How many ducks and geese use the Platte River and nearby wetlands during spring migration?

A. Between seven and eight million.

Q. In what city was the 911 system for emergency communications developed and first used?

A. Lincoln.

———∞∞———

Q. What is the primary source of water for the Platte River west of the mouth of the Loup River?

A. Rocky Mountain snow melt.

———∞∞———

Q. How many miles of trails does the Indian Cave State Park offer for cross country skiers?

A. Twenty.

———∞∞———

Q. When did the Park and Game Commission declare its efforts to save the Canada geese a success and disband its program?

A. July 1997.

———∞∞———

Q. What was the hobby of Gen. Curtis LeMay who headed the Strategic Air Command from 1948 to 1957?

A. Tinkering with sport cars.

———∞∞———

Q. Where was the home of John Lundgren, considered the most prolific maker of duck decoys in Nebraska in the 1920s and 1930s?

A. Axtell.

———∞∞———

Q. What color is the crown of the adult sandhill crane?

A. Red.

Q. What is the scientific name of the American buffalo once found wild in Nebraska?

A. *Bison bison.*

Q. What University of Nebraska faculty member was a pioneer in air conditioning?

A. A. A. Luebs.

Q. The first recorded stocking of fish in Nebraska was the accidental dumping of a train carload of bass into what river in 1875?

A. Elkhorn.

Q. What is the state rock?

A. Prairie agate.

Q. Who was the wildlife manager, killed in a plane crash while surveying deer, for whom a fifteen-hundred-acre refuge near Plattsmouth is named?

A. Randall W. Schilling.

Q. What is the largest dune field in the Western Hemisphere?

A. Nebraska Sand Hills.

Q. Where is the world's largest indoor rainforest?

A. Omaha's Henry Doorly Zoo.

Q. What is the common name of the blue chalcedony, the official state gem?

A. Blue agate.

———∞———

Q. What is the company that makes communications equipment on the site of the former Omaha Works of Western Electric?

A. Lucent Technologies.

———∞———

Q. What museum displays a two hundred-pound land tortoise, estimated to be between 8 and 9 million years old?

A. Lincoln County Historical Museum.

———∞———

Q. What Nebraska City tree nursery is the oldest functioning nursery in the Forest Service and produces 3.5 million seedlings each year?

A. Charles E. Bessey Tree Nursery.

———∞———

Q. What archeological site near Crawford contains bones of more than six hundred bison that are approximately ten thousand years old?

A. Hudson-Meng Bison Bonebed.

———∞———

Q. What museum holds the Toren Gallery of Ancient Life, which includes a touchable, two billion-year-old fossil?

A. University of Nebraska State Museum.

———∞———

Q. What four-day event in Grand Island celebrates the flocking together of 80 percent of the world's sandhill crane population on the Platte River?

A. Wings Over the Platte.

Q. What is the state grass?

A. Little bluestem.

———————

Q. What percentage of Nebraskans live in an area where drinking water is in compliance with federal standards?

A. 99 percent, the third highest among the states.

———————

Q. In 1971, what University of Nebraska paleontologist discovered fossil remains of prehistoric rhinoceroses at Ash Fall Historical Park near Royal?

A. Michael Voorhees.

———————

Q. What retired general who was the last commander of the Strategic Air Command near Omaha has become an ardent anti-nuclear activist?

A. Lee Butler.

———————

Q. Who are the parents of Nebraska's first quintuplets, born July 7, 1998, at University Hospital in Omaha?

A. Jeff and Karla Jansen.

———————

Q. How much did the widow of noted chemical engineer Donald Othmer bequeath to the University of Nebraska?

A. $125 million.

———————

Q. What is the function of a new thirteen-story, $61 million addition to the University of Nebraska Medical Center in Omaha?

A. Organ transplants.